SPEAK
UP

THERESA MILLER has 30 years' experience as a journalist, media adviser, presenter and corporate trainer. She coaches people from all industries to confidently share their expertise and experience with a wider audience. As a television journalist, Theresa worked as a reporter, producer and presenter in Britain, Switzerland and Australia, including Sky News (UK), *Good Morning Britain*, CNN and the Zurich-based *European Business Channel*. In Australia, she worked for the ABC, SBS, Channel Nine and Channel Seven, including reporting for *Australia's Most Wanted*. She is the author of two other books, *Making Babies: Personal IVF Stories* and a novel, *The Spin Doctor's Wife*. She has written for several publications, including *The Australian*, *The Medical Republic* and *The New Daily*. She has lectured in media at UNSW and the University of Sydney. Theresa has a bachelor's degree in Journalism from the University of South Australia and a master's degree in Creative Writing from the University of Technology, Sydney.

'Theresa Miller is very good at what she does: training people to speak in the media. *Speak Up* is not a substitute for her coaching, but it does provide a step-by-step guide to getting your message across. Miller manages to cover everything, from having an idea to tailoring it for the audience. And it's a quick, easy and informative read.'
Richard Aedy, podcaster and former Radio National presenter

'Theresa Miller sets out clearly and concisely how to deliver a speech and handle a media interview. I loved that she not only explained what to do in these situations, but also what not to do. The book is an outstanding guide to public speaking from an experienced practitioner.'
Tim Dunlop, speaker and author of *Why The Future Is Workless*

'Great speakers aren't born, they're made: here's a clear guide for anyone who wants to ditch the nerves and conquer public speaking.'
Catherine Fox AM, commentator, award-winning journalist and author of *Breaking the Boss Bias: How to get more women into leadership*

'Theresa Miller has been working at the media coalface for decades and knows better than most how to cut through the jungle of noise, nonsense, and hollow corporate spin. *Speak Up* is jam-packed with smart, simple, practical tools to empower even the most reluctant speaker. Far from complicated, great communication flows easily when you understand the core principles of storytelling, as laid out in this highly accessible book. Once read, it's a book you will frequently return to for a pep talk reminder!'
Virginia Haussegger AM, award-winning journalist, gender equity advocate and author of *Unfinished Revolution: The feminist fightback*

'I wish I'd found *Speak Up* at the beginning of my public speaking journey.'
Dr Terri Janke, Indigenous lawyer and author of *True Tracks: Respecting Indigenous knowledge and culture*

'*Speak Up* is refreshingly practical. Miller doesn't just tell you to "be confident" – she provides the actual structures, from the "point, reason, example, so what?" framework to crisis communication protocols tested in real-world situations. Her examples range from scientists explaining pandemic modelling to lawyers navigating media scrutiny, making the advice relevant across a range of areas.

For business professionals, researchers, cultural leaders, and anyone working at the intersection of public service and expertise, this book offers something rare: a path to amplifying your impact without compromising your integrity. Miller reminds us that silence isn't noble – it's a missed opportunity to inform, inspire, and influence change. *Speak Up* gives the tools to share your message effectively.'

Kim McKay AO, Director and CEO of the Australian Museum

'As a journalist, I've interviewed hundreds of people who know their subject inside out but freeze the moment a microphone appears. *Speak Up* explains exactly why that happens – and, more importantly, how to fix it. Theresa Miller writes with the authority of someone who has lived on both sides of the media divide: as a reporter under deadline pressure and as a coach helping people survive those encounters with their credibility intact.

What I value most about this book is its honesty. Theresa doesn't glamorise the media or oversimplify public speaking. She understands the fear, the mistrust and the very real consequences of getting it wrong – because she's been there. Her advice is practical, grounded and refreshingly free of jargon, shaped by decades in newsrooms, studios and training rooms across Australia and overseas.

This is not a book about turning experts into slick performers. It's about helping smart, thoughtful people communicate clearly, ethically and with confidence when it matters most. For journalists, academics, leaders and anyone who believes facts still matter in public life, *Speak Up* is both a reality check and a generous guide.'

**Sandra Sully AM, senior journalist and presenter
for 10 News First, Sydney and Queensland**

SPEAK UP

THERESA MILLER

NEWSOUTH

UNSW Press acknowledges the Bidjigal people, the Traditional Owners of the unceded territory on which the Randwick and Kensington campuses of UNSW are situated, and recognises the continuing connection to Country and culture. We pay our respects to Bidjigal Elders past and present.

A NewSouth book

Published by
NewSouth Publishing
University of New South Wales Press Ltd
University of New South Wales
Sydney NSW 2052
AUSTRALIA
https://unsw.press/

 A catalogue record for this book is available from the National Library of Australia

ISBN: 9781761170447 (paperback)
         9781761179358 (ebook)
         9781761178610 (ePDF)

Cover design Thérèse Leuver
Cover image shutterstock
Internal design Josephine Pajor-Markus

All reasonable efforts were taken to obtain permission to use copyright material reproduced in this book, but in some cases copyright could not be traced. The author welcomes information in this regard.

Contents

I raise up my voice – not so that I can shout,
but so that those without a voice can be heard.

– Malala Yousafzai

Introduction

Cast your mind back to the beginning of 2020. The news was reporting a strange new virus spreading across the globe. It hadn't yet reached our shores, or so we thought. The *Ruby Princess* cruise ship was still on the high seas. It would be weeks before it docked at Sydney Harbour, unburdening its infected passengers and crew onto our cities' streets. Our politicians seemed as confused as the rest of us. Journalists were frantically casting around for experts to shed light on this apparent threat.

Meanwhile, at UNSW, Associate Professor Deborah Cromer, a researcher and mathematical modeller in infectious diseases, was observing the unfolding scenario with a scientist's curiosity. After years of studying similar viruses in textbooks and academic reports, she could hardly believe that an actual pandemic had leapt off the pages and was playing out on the world stage in her lifetime.

Journalists from around the country rang, emailed, texted her – 'Please can we interview you? What's the likely trajectory of this virus? How many people do you expect will die or fall sick? How long will this last? What can we do to protect ourselves? Please call back asap.'

At first, Cromer politely declined. She was a serious academic, not a media spokesperson. Journalists were not to be trusted. Unlike numerical data, their behaviour was unpredictable. She went back to crunching numbers and the media found alternative interviewees. But then Cromer heard and read news reports quoting wildly inaccurate data about predicted infection rates. Speculation was rife and often wrong. The numbers were alarming and mostly way off track. It was then that this career academic felt compelled to speak up. With her unique expertise, she knew she had a responsibility to set the record straight and allay the public's fears.

Cromer sought advice from the university's communications department, and they set up a few interviews with respected journalists. By the time I met her at UNSW for her one-on-one media training session, she'd already successfully conducted several interviews. In our session together, we refined her performance. I interviewed her on camera about the coronavirus and played back the interview, showing her what she'd done well and how she could improve next time. We workshopped her objectives and structured her key messages in a logical way that was easy for her lay audience to follow. We discussed tactics to stay on track when the questions strayed into potentially dangerous or irrelevant territory or when the journalist engaged in unhelpful speculation. Together we mapped out a plan to deliver a clear, concise and accurate message.

Cromer is now a frequent media interviewee. She also presents public science forums to school students to educate and debunk myths. She's doing her part to inform the public, influence policymakers and inspire the next generation of scientists. Her media appearances also boost her profile and that of the university, which is useful when applying for funding, grants or attracting industry investment and collaboration.

Unfortunately, despite their wealth of knowledge, many subject matter experts resist stepping up to the microphone. They remain silent and instead rail against the media and the general public's ignorance when speaking to their peers at conferences or dinner parties. But their silence isn't noble. It doesn't help them, the public or their cause.

I understand their reticence. I grew up watching TV commercials featuring BP's 'Quiet Achiever' – that imaginary, hardworking Aussie bloke who didn't ask for praise or acknowledgement but simply got on with the job. They were the values at the time.

My grandmother used to say: 'An empty vessel makes the most noise.' This was possibly an attempt to silence her chatty granddaughter; however, the notion stuck. An empty rainwater tank makes a loud sound if you beat on its side. If it's full of water, it has a muted tone. This extends to a person whose head is full of knowledge and who maintains a dignified silence as opposed to an empty-headed fool who natters about nothing.

Many experts still insist their work speaks for itself and don't feel the need to talk to journalists, speak on panels and podcasts or present at conferences and events. They don't even speak up about their achievements at work and potentially miss out on well-deserved promotions. Unfortunately, it's not always the smartest or hardest-working person who's promoted or given opportunities; it's the one who is most memorable and visible. The days of Australia's 'Quiet Achiever' have long gone. And while we can't stop the loud hailing of empty vessels, we can dampen their negative effect with the voices of reason.

I believe it's the responsibility of experts and experienced professionals and leaders everywhere to offer well-informed reactions and opinions to issues that affect us. If you have knowledge or first-hand experience that could help solve problems, whether it's how to sustainably and cost-effectively power our homes, combat gender-based violence, keep our kids safe online or improve our health/legal/political systems, then it's time to speak up.

As a media and presentation skills trainer, I've interviewed and coached thousands of spokespeople from all industries: CEOs to NGOs, athletes to celebrities, scientists to philanthropists, social workers to tech entrepreneurs. What astounds me is that while many of them have in-depth knowledge, experience and insight into possible solutions to pressing problems, such as climate change, homelessness, mental health and cancer, we don't often hear their voices in mainstream media.

It's not only what we see and hear in the media that's a problem. It's what we *don't* see and hear that's the bigger problem. Now, more than ever, we need accurate information from experts, whether they're lawyers, scientists, AI engineers, psychologists, farmers, authors or economists. We need complex ideas explained simply and objectively. We've had enough of ill-informed media commentators and AI-generated junk filling our news feeds, eroding our confidence in the truth and undermining democracy.

Sometimes, when I explain what I do for a living to my journalist friends, some seem to disapprove. 'Why have you switched from journalism to media and presentation skills training? You're encouraging people to evade our questions?'

'On the contrary,' I say. Media training levels out the playing field so that it's not only the journalist with all the tricks up their sleeve. If you understand how the media works and what makes a good story, you'll become a better spokesperson, and you won't be caught like a deer in the headlights when you're asked to speak to journalists, give a presentation or pitch an idea or offer.

This book gives you the tools to speak confidently and control the conversation rather than being derailed by an interviewer with an agenda. Preparation is key, because whether you're going for a job interview, speaking to a journalist or fielding audience questions on a panel or during a presentation, you don't want to be scrambling for an answer when you're feeling nervous and under pressure. Ideally, you need prepared responses delivered clearly, correctly and succinctly. These are also essential skills for when you're speaking to clients, pitching for new business, seeking a job promotion or encouraging would-be investors, sponsors or collaborators.

Even in today's noisy world of social media, an interview with a respected media outlet can cut through. Played right, it will help boost your brand and profile, promote your cause or research, celebrate your hard work and success, debunk myths, educate and inform, attract staff and customers, and sometimes even influence policymakers.

When my daughter was in year 6, then prime minister Malcolm Turnbull visited her primary school. He met the leadership team in the library for morning tea and asked if they had any questions. My daughter wanted to know what he was doing to save the Great Barrier Reef. Meanwhile, her classmate Tanna Bellear asked why the continuous glucose monitor (CGM) for children with type 1 diabetes was so expensive and not subsidised on the Pharmaceutical Benefits Scheme (PBS). 'I've recently been diagnosed with type 1 diabetes and am fortunate enough that my family can afford the CGM, but I want all kids in Australia to be able to afford it if they need it,' he said to the prime minister.

Tanna was a talented soccer player, and without medication and monitoring he was not always well enough to train. To Turnbull's credit, he invited Tanna to his office to discuss the matter further. As a result of speaking up, the CGM is now on the PBS, and that confident young man is in Germany playing semi-professional football. He continues to manage and monitor his condition daily.

If a 12-year-old can bravely step up and put his case to the prime minister, then we too can speak up when we see an injustice or identify a challenge that needs fixing.

The first part of this book focuses on presenting, whether it be to a small group of work colleagues or a stadium of thousands. The second section is about staying in charge of a media interview. Many of the principles of communicating clearly and effectively are similar.

Being a confident presenter and media spokesperson is not the domain of a handful of polished extroverts with winning smiles and the gift of the gab; it's achievable for anyone who has something worthwhile to share. If you master these techniques, you'll acquire life skills that will not only empower you to motivate and educate others but also boost your career, elevate your cause and open new doors. Drawing on my experience as a TV reporter, actor, presenter and trainer, this book gives you proven techniques to use when presenting at work, facing a job interview, responding to media questions, speaking on a panel or podcast, or pitching an idea. It's my sincere wish that you use these tools to shine a light on your expertise, for the benefit of yourself and others.

If you don't speak up, you risk becoming invisible and your important work and experience may fly under the radar. You'll be unheard, unseen and your gifts will remain unopened. As the late, great Nelson Mandela said: 'Your playing small doesn't serve the world.' So, take charge, step up to the microphone and be heard.

CHAPTER 1

Why speak up?

If you're lucky enough to be passionate about your work or cause, why not simply keep your head down and get on with it? Why get up on a soapbox and crow about it? Isn't that a little egotistical? Surely your work should speak for itself. Sadly, this isn't enough, and we need to broadcast our message for several good reasons.

Firstly, you may want to share your expertise with a wider audience to inform and educate the public and debunk myths. Unfortunately, a lot of ill-informed or uninformed media commentators are spruiking their opinions with little knowledge to back them up. As a subject matter expert, you have the opportunity to combat misinformation. Speaking about your work will create opportunities and could even save the planet.

For more than a decade, Belinda Ferrari from the UNSW School of Biotechnology and Biomolecular Science and her team have analysed and tested a rare bacterium that lives in extreme cold on virtually thin air – hydrogen, to be precise. The scientists hope the microbes might one day help extract greenhouse gases from the atmosphere while revealing the effects of climate change on the polar regions.

In 2019, she and her team went to Casey Station in East Antarctica to check on the health of the bacteria communities. Sadly, climate change had taken its toll, and their numbers had declined drastically. Ferrari's team wanted to return to Antarctica to test their hypotheses about why this was happening, but research trips to the South Pole don't come cheaply, and there's stiff competition for places at the Australian Antarctic research stations.

Ferrari has missed out on several rounds of funding grants to scientists with higher profiles. Consequently, she has stepped up to speak on panels, present at conferences and talk to the media about the significance of their work. 'Antarctica is warming at an alarming rate, and most conservation strategies don't include microbes. These organisms are vital to the carbon cycle and are the building blocks of life. We can't afford to lose them,' Ferrari said. 'Even though they're very small, they carry out important functions for the health of the planet.'

You too may feel small and sometimes invisible, but unlike those microbes, you can't live on thin air. Like Ferrari, if you believe your cause is significant, speak up. Doing this both within your organisation and publicly can help you:

- attract clients, customers, investors and staff
- boost your career profile and chances of promotion
- celebrate your hard work and successes
- combat misinformation about your industry, research or cause
- inform and educate people
- change public perceptions

- win grants and awards
- influence policymakers
- inspire the next generation.

In fact, not taking up opportunities to share your expertise and stories can be quite detrimental. We all know people who are not necessarily the best at what they do but who are more visible in their field and attract more clients, customers and attention.

Years ago, I attended Latin and ballroom dancing classes at a local school hall. We learned to dance the samba, cha-cha, jive and rumba. It was the highlight of my week. We put on a concert at the end of the year for our friends and families. I soon discovered from my classmates that our teacher, Sally (not her real name), was once one of Australia's most talented and awarded dancers in her field. In her early 20s, she and her dance partner were ranked 13th in the world. Her mother worked three jobs to send them to London to learn from the best teachers and enter competitions. They spent almost all their money on costumes and lessons and sometimes went without decent meals. Sometimes they were so skint they raided the one-pound coins from shopping trolleys to buy Big Macs for dinner. Not an ideal diet for competing athletes. But Sally and her dance partner worked hard and impressed the European judges in a very competitive arena. So, what was Sally doing teaching a bunch of beginners in a school hall in Sydney? Thankfully for us, she was also a talented teacher, patient, a stickler for technique, a clear communicator and a lot of fun. But her classes were small. Sometimes there were only three or four of us. She didn't advertise or market herself, and eventually she left to have a baby and didn't return.

Meanwhile, I sought out another dance course. Through social media I found a salsa class nearby. It was run by 'Cameron', who'd left his corporate job to teach salsa with his South American girlfriend, who was a decent dancer. His dancing skills were basic, but he was amiable, a good businessman and even better at marketing. He posted videos of his classes on Instagram and Facebook, offered discounts to bring along friends, held social events and talked on radio and TV about the benefits of learning salsa. His business grew until he opened multiple dance classes around the city. Cameron became a salsa competition judge, an ambassador for salsa clubs and was sought by journalists and podcasters reporting on Sydney's social dance scene.

I don't begrudge Cameron's success for a minute. In fact, I celebrate his achievements. But I can't help but feel frustrated for Sally, who, although a superior dancer and a gifted teacher, did not create the same opportunities for herself. You might say that not everyone wants to put themselves out there and build their profile and business. But being known for what you're good at and passionate about can open doors and offer more options. What's the point in hiding your light under a bushel? We need everyone's talents. Don't keep them to yourself.

What makes a great presenter?

When I ask clients in a presenting workshop who they think is a great speaker, they often mention several celebrities, including former US president Barack Obama. It's useful to look at what great speakers do and learn from them, but it's not always useful to compare yourself to them.

London-based Stephen Watson is a former BBC journalist who, like me, coaches clients to communicate in public forums. He was fortunate enough to see Barack Obama speak in person at the COP 26 in Glasgow. Stephen recalls there'd been a string of uninspiring speakers before the former president strode onto the stage.

'Then Obama comes in and lights up the room. He was electric. He has this wonderful ability and technique to engage audiences,' Watson says. But he assures his clients that it's unlikely Obama was just born lucky.

'Sure, he's good-looking and tall – that helps – but if you search for his early speeches in Chicago when the presidency was not even a dream, the reality is, he wasn't very good. His speeches were quite underwhelming. He has been on a journey and has taken this skill seriously and worked at it,' Watson says. 'I believe everyone can learn to speak well. It's a set of life skills that will elevate you, but you've got to train and prepare like an athlete.'

It's not realistic to believe that great communicators deliver tremendous speeches spontaneously. They have been working on their subject matter and the art of performance for years.

Many communication experts preach the 70/30 rule, which means 70 per cent of the impact of your presentation comes from your non-verbal cues and 30 per cent from the actual words. Stephen believes it's probably more like 50/50. He gives his C-suite clients this pep talk before they speak publicly: 'The last time you prepared for a speech or board presentation, you probably spent all your time on your slide deck and not on how you will show up and light up the room. You can learn techniques and mannerisms to add to the theatre and impact, but ultimately, be authentic, not an actor. Be the best version of you.'

Australian politicians and business leaders tend to be more casual than their American or British counterparts, which reflects our way of life. But can they appear too laidback when speaking or debating publicly? In the lead-up to the 2025 election, the Treasurers' debate was broadcast live on Sky News. This was an opportunity for voters to see Treasurer Jim Chalmers and Shadow Treasurer Angus Taylor debate how they'd handle the economy. On ABC TV's *Insiders* program, *Australian Financial Review* journalist Michael Stutchbury had some frank feedback for both politicians on their presenting styles:

> At 7.30 pm, Jim Chalmers needs to watch his 5 o'clock plus shadow, otherwise he'll end up looking like Richard Nixon in the 1960 debate with JFK. On the other hand, Angus Taylor spent most of the debate with one hand in his pocket. He looked like he was lounging his way through the debate. He needs to take both hands out of his pockets so they can go on the steering wheel and steer the economy through.

So, what do stand-out speakers like Barack Obama do when they present? Here are some of the characteristics that define a great presenter:

- makes a good first impression
- has a compelling mission or purpose
- grabs your attention from the start
- speaks clearly and succinctly
- is knowledgeable, credible and confident
- is passionate and enthusiastic
- is calm and empathetic
- speaks in plain English – doesn't use jargon and acronyms
- speaks fluently with no 'ums' and 'ers'
- is engaging, entertaining and uses humour
- explains complex concepts simply using analogies and examples
- inspires the audience to act or change
- uses a clear, logical structure
- understands the audience's challenges and presents realistic solutions
- uses relevant quotes and statistics
- tells an interesting story
- has open body language and maintains eye contact with the audience
- is well prepared
- is natural and authentic
- finishes with a strong call to action.

This is a long list and might seem daunting to someone new to presenting. The truth is, it's almost impossible to be all those things at any one time. Some of these will come naturally to you and others you'll need to work on. Some may take a lifetime to master. Perhaps the best place to start is to look at some of the barriers to being a good presenter. These include:

- nerves
- lack of preparation
- unclear speech – mumbling, speaking too fast/slow
- overusing 'ums' and 'ers'
- over-reliance on complex, hard-to-read PowerPoint slides
- lack of a clear, logical structure
- overuse of technical jargon and acronyms.

We'll look at many of these later, but first, let's tackle the most common barrier – nerves.

Combating nerves

Nerves before a presentation or interview are normal. You'd be unusual if you didn't feel them. According to *The Book of Lists* by David Wallechinsky and Amy Wallace, 41 per cent of people interviewed said they feared public speaking, while only 19 per cent feared death. This led to the misreporting that people fear presenting more than dying. While this is not quite true, it didn't stop comedian Jerry Seinfeld from observing that 'most of the mourners at a funeral would prefer to be in the coffin than giving the eulogy'. Okay, so it makes a good gag, but let's dig deeper as to what's going on.

Anxiety about speaking publicly or speaking in general is also called *glossophobia*, from the Greek *glossa,* meaning tongue, and *phobos,* meaning fear or dread. And while we're speaking Greek, here's another relevant one: *scopophobia* – an intense or irrational fear of being watched or perceived by others.

In the US, more than 60 per cent of university students claimed they feared speaking in public. However, the researchers acknowledged these results were 'self-reported', meaning the students observed their own reactions to the request to give an impromptu speech. Their barometer was their physiological reactions, such as sweaty palms, butterflies in their stomach, dry mouth and elevated heart rate. These are common symptoms of anxiety. They're also present when we're 'tingling with excitement'. Perhaps you remember your racing pulse on your first significant date, your wedding day, an exhilarating speed boat ride or the anticipation of meeting your idol. The body makes no distinction between nervousness and excitement. It's your mind that interprets these signs. You can reframe your symptoms and tell yourself you're excited about the invitation to speak about your research, project or a campaign you care about.

Ideally, you want to harness that adrenaline to give your delivery energy instead of letting it cripple you. By practising this reframing, you'll eventually associate sweaty palms and a fluttery tummy with eagerness rather than apprehension.

It's also heartening to know your audience perceives only a fraction of what's going on in your body. How often have you given a speech at a friend's birthday party and said to your partner, 'Gosh, I was *so* nervous,' and they looked surprised and said, 'Well, you certainly didn't show it!'

Most people who come to see you speak want you to succeed. Have you ever heard anyone say: 'I'm going to see that bestselling author speak at the Writers' Festival because I want to see how nervous she is?' No! You're paying good money to see them because you believe they'll have something wise, humorous or insightful to say. Seriously, you wouldn't worry about what people thought of you if you knew how little they actually care. We are far too busy worrying about ourselves to imagine what might be going on inside the guest speaker's mind.

Our audience is always tuned into WIIFM, the world's most popular radio station: What's In It For Me? Audience members hope your presentation will deliver a nugget of information to somehow improve their lives, make them wiser, richer, more popular. They're looking for solutions, salvation and distractions.

We are constantly filtering our intake of information based on whether something is useful and how it makes us feel. Big Tech algorithms know this all too well. If your Instagram feed is full of bouncing baby goats and quick mid-week recipes, it's because that's what amuses you or solves a time problem.

One of the best strategies for combating nerves is to focus on the audience instead of yourself. Rather than asking, 'What am I going to say and what will they think of me?', ask yourself, 'What can I give them that will be beneficial? How can this be of use to them?' The better you know your audience, the easier it is to give them what they want. Put yourself in their shoes and address their concerns, pain points and dilemmas. When you see your presentation as a gift or a service, then it takes the focus off you and flips it to the audience.

John Demartini is a successful public speaker and author. For more than 50 years, he's given an average of 300 to 350 presentations every year, around the world, on a vast range of topics. For decades, he's helped people break through their anxieties about public speaking. I interviewed him via Zoom while he sailed past the majestic Milford Sound in New Zealand in his residential cruise ship. Demartini says one of the main reasons we fear speaking is that we compare ourselves unfavourably to audience members. We mistakenly believe they are more knowledgeable, successful, attractive or better educated than us. 'The second you do that, you become self-conscious, and you're not thinking about what you want to say in serving people,' Demartini says. 'You're worrying about yourself. And if you think about yourself, you can't speak. You need to think about your audience and the message you want to give them.'

Preparation is key

For some lucky people, preparation is scribbling a few notes on a beer coaster seconds before giving a speech at a wedding or speaking to a reporter. Those people are rare. For others, it might be researching, writing and rehearsing your speech in the mirror. It's different for everyone. You need to prepare to a level where you are comfortable. Remember how you felt going into an exam or your driving test? If you hadn't studied, you would have been more nervous than if you'd reviewed all the material and practised several past exams.

I used to be a media adviser for a lord mayor, and we would constantly practise his key messages on the way to an interview. 'If you are asked about transport, what do you say? If you are asked about the budget, what do you say? If you're asked about security, what's your answer?' By the time it came to the actual interview, he was so comfortable that his words flowed naturally.

Demartini also attributes his ability to speak fluently to a lifetime of preparation. 'These days, I don't ever do a verbatim speech. I just have some idea. I usually start with a theme and maybe three or four bullet points, and I go from there. I've been doing it for so long,' he says.

For us mere mortals who only present once or twice a year, that's probably not helpful advice. I pushed Demartini for more preparation tips. He confessed he only speaks about what he knows thoroughly and always prepares more content than he needs. 'If I have a 30-minute speech, I have two hours of material. If I have an hour speech, I prepare for four hours. If I have an all-day speech, I have four days of material ready. I'm always four times more ready than the request,' Demartini said.

Like Demartini, I always research my clients and their topics thoroughly before I run a media or presentation skills session. Some would say I overprepare, but I don't think there's any such thing. Do your homework to the level that makes you feel comfortable.

Build on past successes

Think about all the times you've done something similar, and it's gone smoothly. Sure, you may not have done a big presentation, but you might have had a successful job interview or spoken at a work seminar and answered questions from your team. Acknowledging that you've already nailed a similar challenge will bolster your confidence.

Visualising success

We know that visualising failure is counterproductive to our performance, and yet we still love to worry. American writer and humourist Mark Twain said: 'I've had a lot of worries in my life, most of which never happened.'

Visualising success, on the other hand, can be very beneficial. It's what elite athletes do when they're training for a high-level competition. In their mind's eye, they see themselves scoring goals. They imagine the ball sailing through the goalposts and the crowds roaring their approval. They visualise being hoisted onto their teammates' shoulders and paraded around like a heroic gladiator. Picturing your interview or presentation going well, and the audience smiling and applauding, can alleviate nerves and put you in a better frame of mind.

Striking a pose

Another tactic many actors swear by is striking a power pose before you step onto the stage. Stand with your feet apart, chest thrust forward, and arms outstretched above your head as if you own the place. Invoke your inner Wonder Woman or Superman. Do this in the wings before you step onto the stage. Our physical body affects our psychological state. Make yourself feel large and in charge.

Smiling

Try a big goofy smile, ensuring it reaches your eyes, to trick your brain into believing that everything's okay. Smiling creates a favourable first impression, helps break the ice, and builds rapport with your audience. Smiling also triggers the release of endorphins and lowers our anxiety levels. And remember, it's rare for anyone to die giving a presentation, although some audience members have complained of 'death by PowerPoint', but we'll get to that later.

Dialling down the nervous system

All the above tactics are useful for garden-variety nerves, but there are times when our bodies betray us. Then it's time to pull out the big guns. And a warning: if you find discussions of bodily functions offensive, you may want to skip this next part.

Scientists claim that from an evolutionary perspective, our bodies cleverly and spontaneously evacuate our bowels or stomachs to make us lighter and faster when we need to flee a predator. Cavemen and cavewomen sprinted across the savannah, on empty stomachs, to escape the gnashing jaws of sabre-tooth tigers and other predators. The modern-day equivalent would be a surfer floating on their board in the ocean, waiting for a decent wave, and then spying the unmistakable shape of a shark's fin less than a metre away. It's enough to strike terror into your ... well, bowels.

One Christmas, I was asked to read the 6 pm news bulletin for Channel Seven in Adelaide while the regular presenters were on holiday. I was excited but nervous about the opportunity. The station's veteran newsreader tried to allay my fears. 'Don't worry, no one watches the news on Christmas Day,' he said. 'And if they do, they're drunk, anyway.' Somehow, that piece of advice didn't help me.

On Christmas evening at around 5 pm, I headed to the wardrobe department to get dressed and have my hair and make-up done. I read and re-read the introduction scripts and rehearsed them out loud, including any tricky pronunciations. I'd checked that the autocue and my microphone were working. The floor manager had adjusted my chair to the right level behind the news desk. I took a sip of water and blinked at the bright lights around the studio, feeling my heart racing. Then, at ten minutes to 6 pm, I felt an overwhelming desire to go to the bathroom. I unplugged my microphone and raced out of the studio, dodging cables, lights and sandbags before pushing open the heavy double doors. The studio technicians called out to me to stop, but I couldn't.

Fortunately, I made it back behind the news desk and on air in the nick of time. I consoled myself that the incident had occurred at ten to six rather than ten past the hour. I apologised later for giving the studio producer a near heart attack. It was all mildly amusing and wildly uncomfortable.

Veteran Canadian–Australian actor of stage and screen, Pamela Rabe, was once asked in an interview: 'What's your advice for people who struggle with being in the spotlight?' She replied, 'It's an adrenaline thing. It's honestly about how your body processes a chemical and nothing to do with self-belief, I don't think. It's chemical.'

Learning how to dial down the sympathetic nervous response and invoke the parasympathetic mode is different for everyone. Meditating for ten minutes beforehand can be beneficial. Taking a brief walk in the sunshine, slowing down your breathing, practising a few yoga moves or simply rolling your shoulders and neck can also work.

Here are two simple exercises you might try before a public speaking event. Stand with your feet hip-distance apart, with your knees soft, and twist your waist side to side, letting your arms swing freely. As you turn, gently tap one arm to your opposite shoulder and the other to your lower back and repeat on the other side. Gradually speed up this exercise and then slow it down. Try 20 repetitions.

Another simple exercise is to touch your toes (or somewhere near) with your knees slightly bent, and then roll your spine back up very slowly, vertebrae by vertebrae. Imagine your vertebrae are beads on a string. Your head comes up last. Roll up and down three times.

My favourite calming technique is box breathing. Inhale for four slow counts, hold your breath for four, then slowly exhale through your mouth for four counts and hold the outbreath for four beats. Visualise four sides of a box as you do this exercise. Repeat these three to four times until you feel centred.

The good news is that after a few successful presentations, you'll feel less nervous and may even enjoy the experience. In any case, it's important to focus on *why* you're speaking. Keep your eye on the prize. Remember your objectives. Speaking publicly can help raise your visibility and career profile. It's an opportunity to influence policymakers, inspire the next generation and celebrate your hard work and success, which can be leveraged when you apply for a promotion.

Seize any chance to speak on a panel or at an industry function to attract investors for your startup, encourage donations to your charity or secure funding for your research. The more a key decision-maker hears your name mentioned in the right circles, the more likely you'll be considered for a grant, funding, an investment or even a research trip to Antarctica.

CHAPTER 2

Preparing your presentation

The key to delivering a great presentation is to give the audience what it wants, not just what you want to tell them. Research your audience and speak their language. It's easier to persuade them of your point of view when you've demonstrated you genuinely care about their cause. Tailor your analogies and examples. If you're invited to speak to a group of year 11 or 12 students about the hazards of vaping, you'll use different language and stories than if you were being interviewed on Radio National, which has an older audience. Be empathetic. If you know your audience has some sort of grievance or pain point, acknowledge that upfront so they can relax and listen to what you have to say.

I was once asked to train a group of footballers on how to best speak to journalists after a match. They'd had some negative publicity and most of the players were young and had little experience answering a sports reporter's questions. They either said, 'No comment,' or mumbled something irrelevant. My boss, who loved the game and had a relationship with the team and their manager, was meant to do the training. But he was sick on the day, and I was the last-minute substitute. I knew zip about rugby league, and I was heavily pregnant. I was not at all who they were expecting. They were also doing the training under duress on their only day off.

As I entered the room, I could feel the hostility radiating from them. The players sat with their arms crossed, and some visibly rolled their eyes and sniggered when they saw a woman in a red dress stretched tightly over an enormous pregnant belly. I had to address the elephant in the room straight away or the session would be a waste of time.

'Media training on your day off? Wow, that really sucks. I'm sorry for you,' I began. 'Oh, and I have a confession. It might look like I have a football stuffed under my dress, but being originally from South Australia, I know very little about rugby league. But as a former journalist, I do understand what reporters are looking for in a story. I can show you how to give quotable quotes so you'll give the media pack what they want and best represent you, your team and your fans.' The tension in the room dropped a little.

The key to winning over an audience, particularly a hostile one, is to research their field of expertise. I didn't know a lot about rugby league, but they appreciated that I'd bothered to read the latest sports stories on their matches. 'So, mate,' I said. 'Last month, when you missed that goal against X and the reporter accused you of letting down the team, what did you really want to say to him? Go on, let's get it off your chest!'

The players had a rant and let off some steam. We workshopped ways to respond and practised interviews on camera. We rehearsed tactics to stay on message and not take the bait from a reporter deliberately trying to get a heated reaction. At the end of the session, they felt better prepared, thanked me and offered me tickets to the next match.

Here are some ways to research your audience, particularly if you're presenting to an organisation or company:

- explore their website
- connect with key players and employees on LinkedIn
- watch the boss's TEDx talk
- read the CEO's or founder's book
- read their handbook or mission statement
- read their annual report
- read their articles and research papers
- follow the organisation and/or leaders on social media
- search for news stories about the organisation and/or key individuals
- listen to their podcast or podcasts their people have been featured on
- interview relevant people in the organisation.

When you know how your audience ticks – their background, preferences, aims and challenges – you'll be in a better position to give them what they want to hear and anticipate objections. If you're one of several speakers, know where you are in the line-up. Find out what the other speakers will be talking about, so you don't repeat the same content.

When it comes to audience research, knowledge is power. If you're pitching to a small group, it will be easier to get inside their heads. If you're presenting to a large group, focus on the key decision-makers.

Most people have a built-in BS radar, and they'll suspect if you're making it up as you go along. Be enthusiastic when it's appropriate. There's no such thing as a boring topic, only a boring speaker. You could be talking about fly-fishing to an audience that cares little for the topic, but if you're genuinely passionate, it will ignite their interest.

Have a clear objective

A good speech is like a pencil; it must have a point. What does your audience want? What are their interests, motivations, objectives, dreams?

If you're speaking to potential investors, you'll want to encourage them to give you money to scale up your business, boost your not-for-profit project or adopt your safety recommendations for their public works program. Whatever your objective, put yourself in their shoes and frame your proposition in a way that appeals to your audience's interests. For example, investors want to make money. If they're philanthropists, they might also want their name associated with a greater good. Think about why they'd be interested in your work and how collaborating or investing will benefit them.

On the other hand, imagine you're speaking to a group of schoolgirls about why they should consider a career in STEM. If you don't put yourself in their mindset, you'll never grab their attention. You could address the barriers that might be holding them back – their pre-conceived ideas that STEM subjects are boring, hard and only for nerds – and then show them the benefits and rewards.

Your objective must be clear. People often say, 'I'm going to present to my team because I just want to update them on what's happening.' That's not a good enough reason. If you want to update your team, send them an email. If you don't have a clear purpose, theme or objective, you'll likely waste your time and your audience's.

At the end of your presentation, do you want people to walk away, grab a coffee and say, 'Well, that was kind of interesting,' and then forget about it 10 minutes later? Or do you want to motivate them to do something specific? Do you want them to nominate you for an award, offer you a promotion, publish your research, buy your book, adopt your recommendations, donate money to your cause or collaborate on a project? The clearer your objective is, the clearer your message, and your audience is more likely to act.

Are you on a mission?

When you're pitching for a research grant to combat food waste or eliminate child poverty, you have a bigger vision than the immediate need to secure the money. John Demartini says when people sense you're on a mission and it's not just about the grant, they will rally around to support you. Your mission is magnetic. 'Success is an illusion of pride. Failure is an illusion of shame. A person who's on a mission doesn't get distracted by either of those. They focus on the mission of contribution to people.'

Ronni Kahn is the founder and visionary of the food rescue organisation OzHarvest. She and her team are on a crusade to fight food waste by rescuing surplus food, feeding those who need it and educating us to use every morsel for the sake of the planet. Ronni never misses an opportunity to share her message, depending on her audience, whether they be corporations, restaurants, supermarkets, farmers, chefs or shoppers. When Ronni asks us to play our part in aiding OzHarvest's mission, it's hard to say no to her energy and passion.

There's no doubt it helps to be passionate about your topic.

Enthusiasm is infectious. But let's be honest, we are not all fortunate enough to be deeply invested in our work. Early in your career, you may be marketing widgets and online services that, quite frankly, you don't really care about. However, you need to pay the rent, and you're determined to learn as much as you can before moving on to a more interesting position or starting your own business.

At this point, it helps to develop a purpose, perhaps unstated, that will drive your pitch or presentation. This will require some soul-searching and honesty. You needn't share it with anyone, but it'll help you stay motivated and on track. For example, you might want to:

- impress your boss
- increase your visibility in your department
- practise your presenting skills
- overcome your fear of public speaking
- improve your chances of promotion
- build rapport with the team you're presenting to
- stand out from the other new recruits
- be considered for other public speaking roles
- grab the attention of your office crush (that can be very motivating!).

Length and timing

Former US president Woodrow Wilson reportedly said, 'If I am to speak ten minutes, I need a week for preparation; if fifteen minutes, three days; if half an hour, two days; if an hour, I am ready now.' If you're not prepared, it's easy to ramble in a presentation, repeat yourself, leave things out, backtrack, include irrelevant details and confuse your audience.

Less is more. If you are asked to speak for half an hour, break it down into smaller chunks. Most people speak at around 130 to 150 words per minute, so you can use this as a rule of thumb when writing your speech. For example, a 30-minute speech will be around 3800 words. However, factor in time for questions, interruptions, tech difficulties and people arriving late. If you're speaking for an hour, consider this timing:

- 5 minutes for your introduction
- 45 minutes for your content
- 8 minutes for questions
- 2 minutes for your closing summary.

You may have to be flexible and wrap up your presentation early or spin it out a little longer if no one asks questions or the next speaker doesn't show up.

A useful tip is to write your presentation and practise it out loud to gauge how long it runs. Then, print out your speech and use a red pen to mark up what is essential – the key points. Use a blue pen for what you'd ideally like to include, such as examples and statistics, and a green pen for what you could say if you have more time, such as anecdotes and references.

Respect other people's time. It's better to finish a minute early than go on a second too long. People might feel resentful and frustrated if your talk goes for longer than you promised.

The time of day you're presenting is also important. At 9 am at the beginning of the week, when people are fresh and caffeinated, you can hit them with more facts, figures and novel concepts. If you're speaking after lunch, your audience will be less alert, so aim to be lighter on the content and more animated in your delivery. Ask your audience questions and encourage discussion.

If you're unlucky enough to be speaking to a group of employees late on a Friday afternoon before a long weekend, you're unlikely to get much valuable input, especially if you're talking to them online. They'll be keen to wrap up as soon as possible. It's best to acknowledge the poor timing and keep your presentation light. Give them a teaser of your content and something to think about over the weekend, then reschedule the following week, when they're refreshed.

When you write your presentation, it's vital to say it out loud. Written content is a different language to verbal expression. Leave room for pauses, questions, laughter and interruptions. We'll explore this in more detail in the chapter on delivery skills.

My best tip for writing a presentation is to write it quickly and then review it the next day. There's something magical that happens overnight. When you look at your presentation with fresh eyes, you can now see its shortcomings. Almost everyone's first draft is a mess. Editing and rewriting is the time to prune the redundancies and repetitions, tighten your structure, strengthen your opener and call to action, and add the colour and stories to make it shine.

Pitching

Pitching usually means to formally propose an offer of your service or goods in exchange for a fee, grant, loan or new business contract. Ironically, the dictionary definition of pitching is also to lurch, erect, throw, hurl, roll, wobble, dive and plunge head-over-heels. Perhaps this is fitting, as standing up in front of a group of people can be a roller-coaster ride of nerves and emotions.

Pitching is more of a two-way conversation than a formal presentation. Therefore, it requires a slightly different mindset. Essentially, your objective is not to sell; it's to communicate. That means you need to do your research, so your offer fits the budget, timing and needs of your audience. Find out what their pain points are, what keeps them awake at night and what their objectives are. That will help you select relevant anecdotes, examples and statistics they can relate to. Put yourself in their shoes. People don't buy features; they buy solutions, trust and relationships.

Creating a pitch

Hollywood is full of dramatic stories about writers pitching their script ideas to movie directors and producers. One is the pitch for the 1986 movie *Alien*. Rumour has it the creators cornered the would-be investors in a lift and said, 'Here's our movie in three words: *"Jaws in Space!"*' The studio bosses apparently signed the cheque there and then. It's highly unlikely it was that easy, but it makes a great story.

Australian actor Margot Robbie managed to persuade

the 80-year-old Mattel company to grant her production company the rights to make the *Barbie* movie. She says the first step was to allay the executives' fears. 'We assure you we want to honour the brand. However, we're not going to shy away from the problematic parts … but it will come from a place of love because we absolutely respect anyone who can make a toy that's still popular after 60-odd years,' Robbie told ABC's *7.30*.

What can we learn from Hollywood about the art of persuading clients, customers, would-be employers or investors that our services, research and ideas are worth backing?

The *Alien* story tells us an ideal pitch is short, sharp and attention-grabbing, while the *Barbie* anecdote reminds us to put ourselves in the shoes of our audience and address their concerns. The other key piece in a successful pitch is having a logical, easy-to-follow structure. You can choose one of the four debating structures, which I describe in detail in the next chapter. The simplest one is 'point, reason, example, so what?'

In a presentation skills workshop, a group of smart women from Snowy Hydro Ltd practised this structure to pitch the four-day work week to their bosses. Their argument went something like this:

Point: The four-day work week would benefit our people and our organisation.

Reason: It would support work-life balance, boost productivity and attract more talent.

Example: Trials overseas have seen a drop in absenteeism, a jump in profits and an increase in job applications to those companies.

So what?: So, we think we should trial the four-day work week next year.

Once you've done your research and structured your argument logically, what happens when you're face-to-face with the client? One common mistake many presenters make is to hide behind their PowerPoint. Remember, you are your best visual aid. Some corporate bosses are finally pushing back against long, boring presentations. Soon after his appointment, ANZ chief executive Nuno Matos reportedly sent a companywide email to staff asking that presentations be restricted to a maximum of five pages or slides because 'limiting the number of pages helps ensure messages are focused … plus it shows respect for everyone's time'. Keynote speaker and CEO of OzHarvest Ronni Kahn never uses PowerPoint to present. She prefers to speak from her heart. She says, 'Less PowerPoint, more power.'

If you insist on using slides, I recommend the 6 x 6 rule. Each slide should contain no more than six bullet points with a maximum of six words. If your slide is too busy, the audience's focus will be split between reading and listening. You want them laser-focused on what you have to say. It's okay to use cue cards with a few prompt words. However, you should maintain eye contact with your audience as much as possible.

As we've discussed, many people feel overcome with nerves before they speak or pitch, even old hands. Rebecca Denholm heads up CTN Asia Pacific – a company that helps organisations tell their stories through videos, events and coaching. Although she's no stranger to pitching for new business, she admits to still feeling nervous at times. 'Own that it's a slightly nerve-wracking process; it shows that it means a lot to you, but don't overdo it. Practise your game face,' Denholm says.

One of the best ways to combat nerves is by rehearsing. Denholm likes to rehearse in front of a mirror or record herself on her phone, and she always practises with her pitching team. You can, of course, practise your pitches anywhere – waiting for the kettle to boil, driving the kids to school, walking the dog, or even while in the shower (the last one might be tricky if you're in a team).

Why not practise your pitching skills with your family, friends and colleagues? You could use them to encourage your teens to eat a healthier diet, convince your family to rent a place by the beach instead of camping, or persuade your friends to watch your movie of choice.

Pitching for a grant

If you're a not-for-profit or startup, you'll know how time-consuming and frustrating it can be applying for grants. It can take days to gather all the necessary documents, testimonials and financial statements to satisfy a rigorous grant application. Sometimes, a face-to-face pitch is easier and more personable. Just as you must meet certain criteria with a written grant, so too must you hit all the sweet spots when appealing in person to an audience or panel. The stakes are high, but it's worth throwing your hat in the ring. There are philanthropists out there who truly want to give away their money.

Let's explore how to pitch to win. Impact100 Sydney is part of a worldwide giving circle that bequeaths $100 000 each year to a charitable project that improves the lives of marginalised communities. To be a member, you donate $1000 a year, either as an individual or part of a small group. Each donation gives you one vote. Around 30 to 50 charities apply for the $100 000 grant every year. Donors choose up to six finalists to pitch at the live Grant Event, and they have seven minutes to persuade the audience to vote for them.

Impact100 Sydney provides training sessions for the finalists to hone their skills. The facilitator guided them through the five Ps of pitching:

1. **Passion**: If you're passionate about your cause, it will shine through. Drive your pitch and excite others. As marketing guru Seth Godin says, 'People don't buy goods and services. They buy relations, stories and magic.'
2. **Purpose**: Why do you need this grant? How will it enable your charity to expand and make a tangible difference? How does it align with your overall mission?
3. **Planning**: You have only seven minutes – choose carefully what to tell your audience and what to leave out.
4. **Practice**: Rehearse, rehearse, rehearse, especially with your pitching partner, so you feel comfortable on the night.
5. **Performance**: It's not just what you say – it's how you say it that will engage your audience. Think about eye contact, gestures, body language and facial expressions.

During the rehearsal, a representative from each charity practised their pitch. Ed from Bandu told the story of a young man from a remote Indigenous community who had excelled at school in sport, art and academia. He won a full rugby scholarship to attend a Sydney university. However, when he arrived in the city, with no family or friends to bolster him, he felt overwhelmed. His studies suffered as a result.

Ed discovered there were many young people in the same predicament. Hurdles such as an unstable wi-fi, not having the bus fare to travel to the city, not having a phone or computer, or simply not understanding how the tertiary system worked created obstacles to furthering their education. He and his colleagues created Bandu to support Indigenous tertiary students. It was his simple story that made Bandu stand out from the other finalists, and they were granted a $100 000 to hire more support staff and offer practical assistance. The young man in Ed's story graduated successfully and returned to his community to help others.

Pitch perfect – tune into your audience

Before you pitch to potential clients, funders, investors or collaborators, it pays to not only research their organisation, and whether they need or want your offer, but also the personalities of their key decision-makers.

There are plenty of personality type tests out there, including the Myers-Briggs system, DISC and the Enneagram. You may have even taken a workplace personality test yourself. Some HR bosses and recruiters swear these tests give them invaluable insights into people's working styles, learning preferences and behaviour. Others caution that these tests can be misunderstood and misread.

But you don't need fancy personality tests to gather useful intel on the people you're pitching to and how they prefer to receive their information. For example, is the key person a 'cut-to-the-chase' kind of character or a 'let's have a chat and get to know each other first' type of person? You may have gleaned this information already from the types of emails they send and how they conduct themselves in work meetings and on the phone. Do they open the email with small talk, or do they simply outline the objectives and meeting agenda in bullet points and never allude to anything personal?

Body language coach Vanessa Van Edwards relates an excruciating anecdote about pitching her TV series idea to a group of studio executives in Los Angeles. At the time, she was experimenting with being more tactile and wrongly assumed that all Californian TV producers were warm and fuzzy types. Upon her first official meeting, the network boss extended his hand to Van Edwards for a formal shake. However, Van Edwards extended her arms widely and said with a broad smile: 'I'm a hugger!' The executive responded tersely with arms crossed. 'I'm not,' he replied. The meeting went downhill from there.

Sometimes you can recover from those awkward first moments. When my first child was a toddler, I went to the ABC in Sydney to talk about a producer role at Radio National. As I fumbled in my bag to find my business card, one of my daughter's well-sucked dummies fell out at the executive producer's feet. I quickly picked it up, a little flustered. 'I'm trying to give it up,' I said, stuffing the dummy back into my bag. Fortunately, the producer laughed and later offered me a job. Knowing she also had young children helped my cause. Otherwise, I might have ignored the dummy and simply handed her my card.

In some cultures, negotiations move much more slowly, beginning with small talk and personal questions to gauge your trustworthiness before getting down to business. Some deals even open with cups of tea and close with vodka shots.

So, before you pitch or present to a small group of decision-makers, find out if they like small talk, tea and hugs, or if they prefer graphs, statistics and 'actionable outcomes' – with no chat and a firm handshake. If you tune into your audience, you have a better chance of hitting the right note.

CHAPTER 3

Structuring your presentation

There are two types of people: planners and pantsers. Planners map out and rehearse their presentation and pantsers fly by the seat of their pants. If your natural tendency is to wing things, you may be surprised to learn there's actually freedom, and a sense of relief, in adopting a structure, but you can still use your 'pantser' skills if the plan fails. As American author and writing teacher Julia Cameron once said, 'Creativity thrives within structure.' Presenting your ideas using a clear, logical structure will provide you and your audience with a useful roadmap. We'll look at several ways to organise your presentation using four common debating structures and two storytelling templates.

Let's start at the beginning. If you can't grab people's attention in the first minute – the magic minute – you'll struggle to keep them on board for the rest of your presentation. Thanks to social media, our attention spans have shrunk. Sometimes, my Gen Z daughters can barely get through a 30-second TikTok video before swiping to the next one.

Be under no illusion that your audience is 100 per cent focused on you all the time. They're probably thinking about what to have for lunch or dinner, checking emails, hoping they won't get a parking ticket or wondering where you bought your shoes. Presenters need to work hard to keep people's attention. Give yourself and the audience a head start with an engaging opener to make the first minute magic.

Attention-grabbing openers

Here are eight ideas you might consider to hook your audience in from the beginning.

1. Acknowledge the audience's problem

This is where your research into the audience will pay off. See chapter 2 for ideas on how to delve into a company or organisation to better understand their goals and pain points. You might want to begin your talk by commending their wins or commiserating with their recent losses. Make sure you know the names of all the decision-makers. People love to feel acknowledged and important.

2. Link your topic to a current news headline

What's making the headlines? Do any of them dovetail with your topic to give it currency and immediacy? Be aware, though, that most headlines are usually negative. Unless you are offering a solution, bad news might turn your audience off from the start. Find something positive – a Logie Award for an Australian actor, the birth of twin pandas at the zoo, a grand final win for their local team or a breakthrough medical treatment. Use the story as a hook to kick off your talk, as long as it's relevant to your overall theme.

Stay away from political comments. When I started out as a cadet reporter at Channel Nine, the chief of staff said to me: 'Theresa, no one in this newsroom or any of our viewers wants to know who you vote for. You are a reporter, not a commentator.' That attitude has changed in the media, but it's still good policy to remain neutral when you present or pitch to an organisation, unless, of course, you're going for a job with a political party.

3. Use an arresting image or a relevant prop for a demonstration

Throughout history, many images and photos have changed people's minds and aroused strong emotions. Think of the iconic photos of Neil Armstrong's first steps on the moon, athlete Cathy Freeman draped in the Australian and Aboriginal flags when she won gold at the Sydney 2000 Olympics, and jubilant scenes in the streets when the end of World War II was declared. Your opening image needn't be life-changing, but it does need to be compelling, thought-provoking and relevant to your topic.

For years, climate experts and concerned locals on Sydney's northern beaches had tried to convince the authorities to build a sea wall to protect properties against storms along the coast. Vast volumes of written reports and data failed to spark action. When a big storm finally washed away sections of beachfront homes, it was the photos of living rooms, kitchens and bedrooms exposed to the elements that woke everyone up. Sofas, beds and kitchen tables teetered on the edge of broken floors. The waves lapped dangerously close.

People could imagine being in those homes. They feared they might be next and demanded action.

Some props don't always inspire the desired outcome. In 2017, when former prime minister Scott Morrison, who was then treasurer, brought a lump of coal into Parliament House to promote mining, not everyone thought it was clever. The PR stunt backfired and was viewed unfavourably around the world. Ideally, your prop will be appropriate, and your image will inspire and move people.

4. Start with a startling statistic or unusual fact

Founder of OzHarvest Ronni Kahn starts her pitches or presentations with some sobering statistics designed to jolt people out of their complacency, such as one third of all our food is wasted and one in five grocery bags will end up in land fill. It's hard to ignore those numbers. Here are examples of other statistics to make people sit up and take notice:

- Two out of three Australians will get skin cancer in their lifetime.
- The Australian cartoon *Bluey* topped the US streaming charts in 2024.
- The new metro tunnel under Sydney Harbour took two years to build and now takes just two minutes to cross.

Make sure your statistics link back to your message. Don't draw too long a bow or you'll lose credibility. For example, when Telstra was first rolling out cables for mobile phone coverage, some regional Australians were cranky about being left out of the telecommunications revolution. A representative of Telstra Countrywide boasted on ABC regional radio that they'd rolled out enough cables to stretch from the Earth to the Moon and back. A local farmer called in and spoke on air: 'Yeah, mate, you might have enough cables to get to the moon and back, but I still can't get mobile phone reception just outside of Dubbo.' Analogies should be relevant, not just cute.

5. Ask a thought-provoking question

When you start with a question, you are inviting the audience's immediate engagement, rather than their passive attention. Here are some ideas to get the ball rolling:

- If you could have any superpower, what would it be?
- If you were the world's leader for a day, what rule would you enact immediately?
- What's the number one threat to your business?
- If you didn't have to work to make money, how would you spend your time?
- What's your worst habit, and what stops you from dropping it?

When you ask a provocative question, give the audience time to think and respond. Ask people to share, if they'd like, and give only positive feedback. Don't judge or criticise. Even if you don't agree, thank them for sharing. This is the beginning of your talk; you want to set up a positive framework.

6. Start with a famous quote

Starting with a relevant, funny or thoughtful quote can set the tone of your presentation and get people thinking. For example, if you're addressing teenagers, you could put up a slide with this quote from Lady Gaga: 'social media is, quite frankly, the toilet of the internet.' You can either say it out loud or simply put it on a slide and refer to it. You might ask for a show of hands if they agree with the quote. Raise your own hand to demonstrate. Use the result to kickstart the conversation. For example, 'Most of you agree that social media is the toilet of the internet, so why do we hang out there?' Say this with a smile and good humour. It can get the conversation rolling. If they disagree with the quote, invite them to give their point of view. Then, depending on the point of your talk, you may segue into your theme of how to use social media responsibly.

The quote must be relatable to your audience. Obviously, a line from the cartoon *Bluey* will work better with pre-schoolers than one from George Bernard Shaw. Also, it doesn't have to be a quote from a famous person. It could be a quote from your CEO or even a satisfied or disgruntled customer whose feedback provoked change.

7. Break the ice with humour

Not everyone's a stand-up comic, but a gentle joke, especially when something goes wrong with the technology, can help break the ice and make people feel more comfortable. Keep your jokes family-friendly so as not to offend anyone. You don't need to have the audience in stitches, just add a little lightness and levity. Laughing will put you and your audience in a better mood.

Using humour can also make your speech more memorable and even persuasive. It can sometimes provide much-needed comic relief when the content is heavy. When she addressed the National Press Club in Canberra, comedian Jean Kitson used humour to talk about menopause at a time when the subject was rarely discussed publicly:

> It's a great pleasure to be the ambassador of menopause.
> I have to say, as far as ambassadorships go, it is not
> one of the more glamorous ones. It is not the New
> York, Paris or Washington of postings. It is rather an
> ambassadorship for one of the very hot, very humid
> postings – unpredictable, volatile, and full of touchy,
> expletive locals.

If being witty doesn't come naturally to you, consider using a well-placed but unexpected image or meme among your PowerPoint slides to add an element of surprise.

If you tell an amusing anecdote, set the scene, build suspense, pause, deliver the punchline confidently and then wait. Don't rush it. Allow the audience time to 'get it'. Use your voice, gestures and facial expressions to add to the comedy. And if your joke flops, own it. 'Mm, that joke was a lot funnier in my head,' or 'You can blame ChatGPT for that one.'

Sometimes, the funniest lines are the call and response with the audience. I once gave a talk about my IVF book and didn't notice that my wrap-around dress was unravelling. My doctor in the front row alerted me by yelling out: 'Theresa, no need to undress, I've already examined you!' Fortunately, the audience laughed with me. In most cases, your audience doesn't want you to feel embarrassed because it'll make them feel awkward too. Even if you're not hilarious, people will appreciate your attempt at building rapport.

8. Tell a personal story or anecdote

Kirsten Banks, who has a PhD in astrophysics and is a descendant of the Wiradjuri people, talks about the Indigenous way of looking at the stars as well as the modern science perspective. On TikTok, she's known as AstroKirsten. This is how she opened her TEDx talk:

> Ever since I could remember, I've enjoyed looking up
> to the stars. It gives me a sense of place and meaning
> within the everlasting universe. And I could be having
> the worst day ever, but when I appreciate the universe
> above me, all those problems melt away for just a little
> while. But we are quickly losing the opportunity to
> enjoy the stars in the sky. We are losing the darkness to
> overbearing bright city lights.

Banks engages us right from the start with a personal anecdote, using emotion and displaying her genuine passion. Then she presents us with the problem.

One of her techniques for evoking emotion is using 'word pictures' or 'bricks of detail'. She talks in concrete terms rather than abstractions about what she sees. Personalisation is a powerful tool in storytelling. It reveals something about the speaker, and no one knows your story better than you do.

Researcher Brené Brown inserts her personal story into her famous TED talk about vulnerability. As a social scientist, she could have simply explained her research in terms of surveys, interviews and analysis. Instead, she revealed her own vulnerabilities. She began her research with curiosity, made an unexpected discovery about the link between shame and vulnerability, and came out the other side with a deeper understanding. This is what we typically call 'The Hero's Journey'. More on that later.

As humans, we love stories. We've been telling them since we could first talk. Sharing stories is a potent way to draw people in. While AI is useful for research, generating ideas and writing standard content, it's not yet a substitute for personal human stories – with all their flaws, quirks and unique perspectives. Tell a personal story to make your presentation memorable.

Debating structures

The following four templates are particularly useful if you're trying to win over an audience to your point of view. If you ever took part in debating at school or university, you might be familiar with them. I've tweaked them for presenting.

Point, reason, example, so what/so why?

The first is this simple structure: 'point, reason, example and so what/so why?' Let's use the topic of a four-day work week to illustrate how it works. Imagine you are talking to an HR conference or employers' association. You might say:

Point: Australian businesses should consider the four-day work week.

Reason: It would foster a better work-life balance.

Example: Employees could spend more time caring for children and their elderly relatives or pursue hobbies and interests that are good for their mental and physical health.

So what/so why?: So, Australian employers should consider trialling a four-day work week.

Point, reason, reason, reason, point

This is what's called the 'three wishes' structure. Most of us can remember three points easily. Let's give it a go using the same topic. This time, you're trying to persuade your boss:

Point: Our organisation should consider a four-day work week.

Reason: Firstly, it would improve employees' work-life balance.

Reason: Secondly, it's proven to decrease absenteeism and improve productivity.

Reason: Thirdly, in the competitive labour market, it would make our company more attractive to talented recruits.

Point: So, we should at least trial the four-day work week.

Point, counterpoint, reason, point

This third structure is useful when someone has raised an opposing point of view, or you want to concede that there are different opinions on the table. You can acknowledge it with your 'counterpoint' and then show why your idea is better in the following 'reason'. Let's give it a whirl:

Point: Australian workers are ready for the four-day work week.

Counterpoint: Of course, it won't suit every industry, especially those in transport, catering or construction.

Reason: But for those in knowledge-based industries, employees can be just as productive in four days as in five, and they can spend the fifth day on life admin and other activities.

Point: Isn't it time we gave employees more flexibility with the four-day work week?

Point, past, present, future, point

Some people call this the 'groom's speech' because it paints a picture of the groom's life in the past as a bachelor, in the present with their partner and their hopes for the future. It's also useful when giving a snapshot of how an issue has evolved. You could use it to outline your department's sales figures over a certain period. Let's see how it works with our topic:

Point: It's time to trial the four-day work week.

Past: Before the pandemic lockdowns, employees were expected in the office five days a week and wedded to

their desks and computers. They needed to be *seen* in
the office.

Present: The lockdowns proved we can be just as
productive working remotely, especially using online
tools and meetings to stay connected. Today, many
of us have chosen to work from home or embrace a
hybrid model, and both companies and employees are
reaping the benefits.

Future: In the future, it will be the norm to fit our work
around our lives rather than the other way around.

Point: So, it's time to adopt the four-day work week.

The beauty of these structures is that you can mix and match
them to suit you. You could add an extra example or reason
to the structure.

Here's a real-life example with Professor Joëlle Gergis
from the Australian National University. She uses the 'point,
reason, example, so what?' structure effectively when speaking
about climate action. You'll notice she puts the example before
the reason. These structures are not set in stone – they are
guidelines:

Point: I think it's important to realise that Australia is
experiencing a lot of climate extremes, things that we
might not have expected to see until a lot later in the
century.

Example: For instance, we just saw the mass bleaching
of the Great Barrier Reef.

Reason: Consequently, 50 per cent of all the corals on
the Great Barrier Reef have been killed by underwater

heatwaves. That's something which we wouldn't have expected to see so soon.

So what?: So, we must understand that we are seeing climate change right now; it's already with us. What we do right now is incredibly important in terms of putting the brakes on.

You can also knit these structures together with linking lines for a longer presentation. Begin with an attention-grabbing opener or hook and then state your position. Outline three points supporting your argument. Then expand each point using one of the structures. Use a linking line to move to the next point until you reach the summary and call to action. This is an example of how you might structure a 30-minute presentation:

- two-minute opener – your hook and attention-grabbing intro
- one-minute statement of your aim – what you hope to prove or illustrate
- one-minute outline of the three key points you'll cover to prove your statement
- 15 minutes of content broken up into 3 x 5-minute mini-presentations expanding on each point
- three-minute summary
- five minutes for questions
- two-minute close with a call to action.

Storytelling structures

When CEOs started telling personal and corporate stories in presentations, I was one of the biggest sceptics. Why would investors and shareholders want to hear executives tell stories? Let them stick to the facts and leave storytelling to the masters.

After seeing several business leaders tell their tales to great effect, I've changed my tune. We all have a story to tell, and it's often the most effective way to communicate your message rather than through a series of dull slides with pie charts.

Historian and author Yuval Noah Harari says stories are the greatest human invention and vital for human societies to function and cooperate. The magic of stories, says Harari, is they create an emotional connection that allows people to gain a deeper understanding of other people's experiences. After all, we think in stories rather than numbers or graphs.

Another expert who understands the magic of storytelling is scientist Dr Karl Kruszelnicki, who explains science in layperson terms. Kruszelnicki says the human brain is uniquely wired to remember stories. 'I use this storytelling trick to turn all my scientific readings from bare facts into true tales, with a beginning, a middle and an end, that I can tell anyone who happens to have a sense of curiosity,' he says.

One of the keys to relating an anecdote well is to use 'bricks of detail'. Not vague terms such as 'I saw a car'. Instead, say 'I saw a tomato-red, 2023 Maserati with Italian-flag racing stripes on the bonnet' or 'I saw a beat-up dark green Toyota Corolla with surf boards on the roof racks'. Activate our senses by describing how you felt or what you heard, smelt, saw and tasted.

When award-winning journalist Anne Connolly produced her first five-part true crime podcast, *The Invisible Killer*, about a suspected killer working in a nursing home, she used specific interview techniques to draw out the drama from her interviewees. Rather than asking complex questions to elicit information, Anne posed simple, evocative questions: 'Where were you when you got that news?' or 'What were you doing?' or 'Tell us how you felt when you heard what had happened to your grandfather?'

This prompted responses like this one: 'I was at home watching TV with my partner, when my phone rang. It was the hospital saying my grandfather was there and he was very ill. I was shocked because I'd just seen him that day and he'd looked so well.' This type of storytelling narrative works well in a long series podcast because it takes the listener on a step-by-step journey.

Even if you're describing a professional story, you can include a decision-making process that changed your company's or research's direction and how it made you feel and where you were when you made that crucial choice.

If you have a longer story to tell, here's my own STORY framework, which is useful if you're trying to paint a picture to persuade people to act or behave differently:

S: Set up/Scenario/Struggle

T: Testing/Trialling

O: Obstacles/Opponents

R: Resolution/Results

Y: Why this matters/What are the implications?

This STORY mnemonic is a handy way to remember all the important elements of an anecdote with a logical flow. The scenario or initial struggle gives us a context for the problem at hand, while the testing and trialling shows us how you've attempted to improve the situation. The obstacles and opponents show the challenges along the way, and the results are the fruits of your labour. The final step illustrates the wider implications or how this lesson can be applied elsewhere. I heard Associate Professor Sara Grafenauer use this structure in a lecture to her health science students:

Scenario: Many people are missing out on the health benefits of nuts because of misinformation.

Testing: Around 180 randomised control trials show the value of eating around 30 grams of nuts on most days.

Obstacles: However, people are still avoiding nuts because they fear they are fattening.

Results: Scientific tests show that nuts can actually help people lose weight, especially when substituted for unhealthy, salty or sugary snacks. Nuts help control cravings and contain many vitamins and minerals. Much of the fat in nuts is not digested.

Why this matters: We don't want people missing out on the nutritional value of nuts because of misinformation.

It's worth taking the time to get the right recipe for a great story. Hollywood is the obvious choice when searching for the successful, large-scale commercialisation of storytelling. While there are many different movie genres — horror, redemption, fable, rags to riches, comedy and tragedy – not all story structures work well for presenters. Unlike a movie director, presenters can't easily introduce flashbacks and multiple points of view to their talk.

A popular choice with presenters is the storytelling structure known as 'The Hero's Journey'. In *The Hero with a Thousand Faces*, American writer and professor Joseph Campbell claimed all plots, from Bible stories to modern film scripts, feature three steps: departure, fulfilment and return. Director and screenwriter George Lucas says he owes much of the success of his *Star Wars* movies to the hero's journey.

The story begins when the hero is called to adventure – for example, Luke Skywalker is summoned to become a Jedi Knight, Harry Potter is invited to attend Hogwarts, Katniss Everdeen is enlisted in the deadly *Hunger Games*. If the hero refuses the call, then an inciting incident will impel them to begin the journey.

Along the way, the hero is given special powers by a helper or guardian (Yoda, Professor Dumbledore, Peeta). At the midway point, the hero finds themselves in a near-death situation. For example, Luke Skywalker, Princess Leia and Han Solo become trapped in a gigantic garbage compactor.

The hero must dig deep to overcome their difficulties. The resolution of the story is the hero's victory over the opponents and their return to society with new knowledge, for the benefit of others. This is the simplified version of the hero's journey: a likeable hero faces a problem, meets a mentor, encounters roadblocks, struggles, experiences a transformation and uses the new knowledge to help others.

You might like to use this structure to tell your own story or that of your organisation. Or you might like to flip it on its head. You could start with the midway crisis as your headline to grab attention and then backtrack to how you found yourself in that mess and what you learned from the experience. Or you might highlight the importance of your mentor and the best advice they gave you. Get creative. Surprise, delight and inform your audience with your story.

Storytelling brainstorm

Jot down some ideas from each turning point you've experienced. When were you catapulted out of your comfort zone by forces bigger than you? Scott Pape, author of *The Barefoot Investor*, writes about when he and his family lost everything in a bushfire and found they were underinsured. He sums up his turning point and the consequences:

> In truth, I spent the first 12 months desperately waiting for everything to go back to normal.
>
> You know what I ultimately learned?
>
> Things don't go back to normal.
>
> Instead, you're forced to find a new normal. And sadly, for many, it's very different from the life they enjoyed before the fires. And all too often these people fall through the cracks and face years of ongoing hardship.
>
> That's what inspired me to spend 2019 becoming a community-based financial counsellor.

Your watershed moment may have been an illness or accident, a divorce, the pandemic, bankruptcy, being made redundant or the death of a loved one that prompted you to choose a different path.

During your journey into this 'new world', what challenges did you face? How did you learn to overcome these? Who were your friends and foes along the way? What was your darkest hour? What kept you going? What did you learn? What advice can you now give to others?

It can be useful to do this exercise with a trusted friend or colleague who may have a different perspective. They may remind you of anecdotes you'd forgotten or didn't realise were significant.

Use a theme

Back when former US president Barack Obama was still a senator from Illinois and on the hustings in the 2008 presidential election campaign, his oratory skills were being noticed. However, his critics wrote him off as a political novice, saying: 'Words don't matter.' Obama turned the criticism into a powerful rebuff:

Don't tell me words don't matter.

'I have a dream.' Just words?

'We hold these truths to be self-evident that all men are created equal.' Just words?

'We have nothing to fear but fear itself.' Just words? Just speeches?

It's true that speeches don't solve all problems, but what is also true is if we cannot inspire the country to believe again then it doesn't matter how many policies and plans we have. And that is why I'm running for President of the United States of America. And that's why we just won eight elections straight, because the American people want to believe in change again.

Don't tell me words don't matter.

Obama uses repetition to reinforce his theme, as well as dramatic pauses after each point to allow his message to sink in. As motivational speaker Dave Carey says: 'A theme is a memory aid; it helps you through the presentation and gives your audience the thread of continuity.' Think about a theme for your presentation to draw your ideas together and make them memorable.

Word choice

Using plain English rather than jargon will ensure everyone can relate to your talk rather than just those from your inner industry circle. Of course, it depends on who your audience is. If you're talking to your academic or legal peers at a conference, you can use all the technical terms you like, but if you're speaking to general audience, you need to translate your tech talk into everyday plain English or you risk alienating people.

I discuss this in more detail in the media interview skills part of the book. You'll know how frustrating it can be when you speak to a doctor, lawyer, executive or IT professional and they use terms and acronyms you've never heard before. Speak to express, not to impress.

What not to say

It's equally important to avoid certain words or phrases that can negate the power of your speech. Here are my top ten pet peeves. It's by no means a complete list, but these are the most common mistakes I see presenters make.

Lacklustre line	What to say instead
'Hello, can you hear me?'	This is an unprofessional and uninteresting way to start your presentation. Ideally, you would have tested the microphone before beginning. Instead, say 'Good evening' or 'Good morning', then pause and launch into one of your attention-grabbing openers.
'I'll keep this short …'	Don't apologise for taking up people's time. It's your job to make your presentation as engaging as possible.
'I've been asked to speak about …'	This sounds like you aren't speaking voluntarily, or the topic was someone else's idea. Instead, own the topic and start with a powerful statement, image or question.

Lacklustre line	What to say instead
'We've run out of time, so I'll go through these next slides quickly.'	Rehearse your presentation so that it falls within the allotted time. If you do run out of time, skip ahead (without apologising) to your summary and compelling closer.
'Close your eyes and imagine …'	Personally, I find this request annoying. It might work with preschoolers or at a meditation retreat, but most adults won't shut their eyes in front of their colleagues. Instead, show an image or describe the scene in detail so we can visualise it clearly.
'Um, look, you know, like …'	These are common filler words. We 'um' and 'er' when we're buying time to think. Pause instead; it's more powerful. A pause helps your audience digest what you've said and flags that you're moving on to a new point. Eliminating filler words can be difficult at first because it's so habitual. The first step is recognising them and gradually replacing them with dramatic pauses.
'I think …'	This sounds like it's your opinion rather than a fact. Instead of 'I think' say that your research shows, your customer surveys reveal, clients tell you, the data confirms, your experience proves or demonstrates.
'To be honest …'	This insinuates you haven't been honest before. Skip this phrase. Cut to your point instead.
'I just want to say …'	Avoid 'just' when possible. It minimises the authority of your message. You're not 'just' saying something, you are delivering an important message. Take charge.

Lacklustre line	What to say instead
'I'm sorry …'	Unless you've made a real boo-boo, such as saying something offensive, misinterpreting your statistics or accidentally putting an inappropriate slide in your slide deck, you probably don't need to apologise. And don't say, 'I'm sorry, this next part is a bit boring.' It undermines your presentation. There is no such thing as a boring topic, only a boring speaker. Don't be sorry. Be informative, inspiring and entertaining.

Closing with impact

The opening and closing statements of your presentation are both crucial. You may have heard of the TV advertising rule of 'primacy and recency', which claims people tend to remember the first and last commercials in the ad break rather than those in the middle.

To take advantage of the primacy effect, hook your audience with an attention-grabbing opener. And then hammer home your message in your closing remarks so it sticks in their minds.

Don't make the mistake of taking questions right at the end – this will dilute your message, and your presentation will simply fizzle out as people dash out the door. If you choose to answer questions, return to the summary and call to action – so that you have the last word. Prepare a transitional phrase: 'I'll take some questions now and then come back with one important change you can make in your organisation today.'

Hopefully, that will keep people glued to their seats rather than scurrying off early.

Remember, you don't have to agree to a Q&A, just because many speakers do it. You could distinguish yourself by not doing it and instead invite audience members to email you their questions or offer to run a 30-minute online Q&A for their executives the following week.

Many people now use Slido or similar apps for audience Q&A. It helps to have a technical assistant filtering and passing the questions to you. If you don't have an assistant, be sure to familiarise yourself with the app before the presentation. Keep your reading glasses handy if you need them.

If you're interviewed on stage by a moderator, give them the final question *you* want to be asked, so you can end with a memorable, punchy closing statement. Here are three suggestions for a strong way to close your presentation.

1. A compelling call to action

Don't make the mistake of ending with 'Thanks for coming' or 'Goodnight'. Otherwise, you've wasted the opportunity to change people's minds and actions. Ask them to do something at a specific time. For example:

- Sign this petition tonight to protect our forests and preserve koala habitat.
- Donate today to the literacy foundation to give children the gift of reading.
- Vote for our candidate on Saturday to advocate for our electorate.

- Download the Beach Safe app to upload your bluebottle photos for this month's citizen science campaign.
- Volunteer for our free trial. Applications close at the end of the week.

2. Answer the question that was set up in the intro

If you asked your audience what the number one threat to their business was and they responded with 'cybersecurity attacks', then give them a solution by the end of your presentation. You want them to associate you with solutions and hope. As poet, author and activist Maya Angelou said, 'people will forget what you said, forget what you did but they'll never forget how you made them feel.'

3. Reinforce key benefits

Sum up the three main reasons people should invest in your research, partner with your company, install your technology system, stock your product, buy your book or sign up for your course. What are the benefits to *them*, not you? Keep it short and snappy, perhaps illustrating those points with images or a before-and-after photo or graph. Paint the picture of how their lives/businesses/health will be improved this time next month or year.

Presenting with an accent

One of the things I love about running workshops is meeting people from all walks of life. However, occasionally participants approach me during the break and say, 'I'm worried about my accent. English is not my mother tongue, and I'm concerned my accent detracts from my message.'

In a presentation skills workshop for a group of highly skilled professionals, one woman became agitated when speaking in front of the group. Although her expertise was rock-solid, she loathed presenting. When I questioned her about it, she said, 'I'm embarrassed about my accent.' Her colleagues and I assured her that her accent did not detract from her message. Rather than being comforted, she began to cry. 'At school I was always teased about my accent. I hated it. So, I vowed never to speak in front of people ever again.'

Please don't make a career-limiting decision based on the judgement of a bunch of eight-year-olds. In my experience, Australians are used to hearing a vast array of accents, and they're quick to adapt.

Executive and team coach Shilpi Joshi agrees. She began her career in the '90s as a speech pathologist, when the trend was to help professional migrants 'minimise their accents'. She says that as our workforce has become much more diverse in the past 20 years, the focus is no longer on 'accent minimisation' but rather improving an individual's ability to be understood. That might mean slowing down, clearly enunciating key words, practising the pronunciation of certain vowels, diphthongs and those pesky 'th' and 'v' sounds. If a word continues to trip you up, she recommends finding easier-to-pronounce synonyms to express that concept.

Speaking up at a job interview

PR strategist Karen Eck runs an online masterclass to help professionals build or renew their career confidence. She says that one of the biggest mistakes people make in their careers is believing their work speaks for itself. Even if you've achieved extraordinary success in your workplace, your colleagues and bosses might forget unless you remind them. Eck says if you don't tell or remind people why they need to do business with you, how will they know?

Remember the story about the gold-medal Latin and ballroom dancer who was Sydney's best-kept secret and the competent salsa teacher who had waiting lists for his dance classes? The difference: self-promotion and marketing. You're probably protesting that such attention-grabbing tactics are beneath you. I get it. But demonstrating how your experience and skills can solve an organisation's problems and make a positive difference needn't feel grubby. It's not just dance teachers who have trouble trumpeting their expertise. A major Australian university recently revealed that many of their associate professors in their Business School struggled to articulate their impact and relevance when interviewing for promotion to professorship.

When the university engaged me to coach their candidates through mock job interviews, I asked one of the decision-makers, 'What criteria make a professorial candidate stand out?' The following check list has been tweaked to apply to most professions:

- can present a strong career narrative
- demonstrates the broader impact of their work in their field or industry
- uses relevant statistics and examples to back up their claims
- is knowledgeable and authoritative in their chosen work area
- uses a clear, logical structure to persuade
- is a creative problem solver
- acknowledges the efforts of their team and colleagues
- highlights how their work aligns with the company's values and strategies.

Let's expand on the first point. What is a career narrative? Many people describe their career journey something like this: 'After uni, I took a job with my friend's dad's company packing shelves, and after a year, I was promoted to distribution logistics. But when the company was sold, I was retrenched and went backpacking for six months until I ran out of money. Then I found a job at company B, and after five years, I was offered a similar role at organisation C with a better salary. Then my partner was transferred to Brisbane, so I got a job up there with corporation D, and now we're back here and I'd like to work for you.'

In this tale, your career resembles a tiny boat tossed at sea, at the mercy of the wind and waves, which, let's be frank, is sometimes the case. However, when you're trying to impress a would-be-boss, tell a story that puts you at the helm and reveals your values, strengths and skills. I'm not talking about embellishing; rather, drawing out the theme in your story and highlighting it to make you shine. Start by asking yourself:

- Who are you?
- What makes you tick?
- What do you stand for?
- What themes drive your work?
- How could your skills/passion/experience benefit the employer you aspire to work with?
- What is your superpower?

Dr Meraiah Foley, an academic and former reporter for *The New York Times*, believes her journalistic training gives her the edge when it comes to communicating to an audience. 'One of the things you learn in journalism is to think about the audience you're writing for,' Dr Foley says. 'I spent most of my time as a foreign correspondent, writing about things happening in a particular country to an international audience, and assessing how much my audience would understand about what I'm talking about, and how much context to include so that what I'm talking about is not only interesting but relevant. So, there's a large amount of translating. A lot of what you're doing as a journalist in your day-to-day is interviewing experts about their area of scholarly or professional expertise and then translating that to a lay audience and connecting it to the bigger picture. So, now as an academic, I'm the subject matter expert, but I still need to ask: "What does my audience know?"'

Foley is an expert in workplace gender equality and researches the organisational, institutional and regulatory factors that either support or undermine gender equality at work. Her superpower is explaining the significance of her research to the growth or decline of the Australian economy, which has made ministers, union leaders and CEOs sit up and take notice. It's won her promotions and considerable grants and funding for her department. Her research has shown that many invisible factors help or hinder gender equality, with flexible working arrangements being one of them.

Foley told me in a phone interview how she angled her pitch to show that the economic consequences of limiting women's progression at work are everybody's business. 'Women in Australia are disproportionately represented in part-time work. So, we have an extremely highly educated and expensive section of the labour market who are vastly underutilised because we don't support flexible work as well as we could,' she says.

Broken down into point form, this is roughly how Foley used logic to engage her audience and win a research grant:

Point: We need to dismantle the barriers that stop women from participating fully at work if Australia is to overcome major economic hurdles.

Reason: Many highly educated women are not working fulltime because their work doesn't allow them to combine work and caring duties.

Reason: The cost of childcare and limited promotion pathways for part-time workers further inhibits their progression at work.

Example: Having a highly educated sector of the population only working part-time is like a farmer buying expensive farm equipment and not using it to its full capacity.

So what?: We need to normalise flexible work arrangements, decrease the cost of childcare and promote rather than punish part-time workers for the sake of our economic prosperity.

It's this last 'so what?' point that's the kicker. This makes the argument relatable and significant for everyone. You can use this structure to explain why your work, research, product, service or campaign is 'everyone's problem or solution.' Analogies, stories and examples are the key to unlocking people's understanding. Join the dots for your audience. Flexible work arrangements might initially seem like a 'women's problem', but Meraiah's research highlights it's an economic challenge for the whole country.

When I was a kid, a teacher wrote in my report card that I was good at 'extrapolating'. I liked the sound of that, even though I had no idea what it meant. It means to draw a bow from one field of knowledge to another to make predictions or deductions. I'm still motivated by figuring out what the bigger picture is or the greater meaning. People will tune out of new information if they're not shown *why* they should care.

In year 11 maths, I begrudgingly learned the trigonometry rules for sine, cosine and tan so I could pass my exams. But I had no clue what their purpose was. It wasn't until I was in my thirties that someone told me trigonometry could be used to measure sound, light and oceanic waves. If our teacher had demonstrated this, I could have at least visualised those different wavelengths, and it would have given them some meaning. When you speak about your work, find the 'so what?' factor to help people understand and care.

Third-party endorsements

When you go to your next performance review, offer evidence that demonstrates how well you're doing in your role. For example, you might present some glowing customer feedback or data showing the $2 million worth of business you brought into the company in the last quarter. 'I'm proud to say that not only did I reach my sales goals last quarter, but I also exceeded them by 30 per cent. We are smashing sales records.'

Visibility coach Karen Eck says you need to give people the key messages or language to endorse you so that when the boss bumps into the sales manager in the lift and asks how Alex is doing, the sales manager can say, 'Alex is smashing it. She brought in $2 million in the last quarter – 30 per cent higher than expected.' That's the power of third-party endorsement.

It's also important to show how your wins match your organisation's values. If your research into recycling plastics sustainably has been published in an overseas science journal, show how it aligns with your department's aim to innovate, tackle global challenges and contribute to the common good.

Voice your ambitions and goals

When I was a young TV producer for Sky News in London, there was another producer who told everyone her number one goal was to be a newsreader. Fast forward seven years and I was watching Star News Hong Kong and lo and behold, there she was presenting the evening news bulletin. Her determination, plus voicing her desire, had paid off. Don't keep your career ambitions to yourself. Yes, you must work hard and be skilled, but no one is going to offer you your dream job if they have no idea that's what you want. You may be passed up for promotions, not because you're not suitable, but because the powers-that-be have never heard you express an interest in them.

'So, tell me a bit about yourself'

This is a job interview question that sometimes makes candidates freeze. They'll often make the mistake of parroting their resume. Yawn. This question is designed to reveal your personality, likes and motivations. The hirer wants to assess whether you'd be easy to get along with and fit into the company's culture. A former hiring manager summed it up this way:

> If I've offered you an interview, I've already reviewed
> your resume. If I ask you to tell me about yourself,
> I want to know who you are as a person or at least
> something that isn't on your resume. I can read. Tell me
> something interesting about you. You built a computer

from scratch. You make quilts for charity. You rehome greyhounds. Anything to make you more personable. While it's not necessary, it's so much easier to work with pleasant people.

When you're asked in a job or promotion interview to 'tell me about yourself,' career mentor Petra Buchanan says it's an opportunity to set the tone early with a one-word description of yourself. 'A one-word descriptor doesn't mean you're going to be able to talk about everything, but it creates an imprint in the mind of the person you're talking to, and you can then hinge the examples you want to impress upon somebody off that descriptor,' Buchanan says.

Examples of one-word descriptors include: disrupter, fixer, connector, strategist, builder, communicator or trailblazer. For example, you might say, 'I refer to myself as a trailblazer because I pioneer new paths and challenge norms.'

Buchanan has been described by a few recruiters as a 'wild card' because her career hasn't followed a predictable trajectory. At first, she was a little offended by the term, but now she embraces it. 'When I talk about my career, I use the opportunity within the descriptor of the "wild card" to say, "I started out here and that piqued my interest in government affairs," which meant I could shift and change into this space.'

'These labels create a visual perception for somebody. And while it seems simplistic, it then allows you to tell that story, and it gives you a simple structure to do that,' she says.

Coming up with the appropriate one-word descriptor for yourself takes some self-awareness, reflection and a brains-trust of friends or colleagues who may see you and your career journey more clearly than you see it yourself. That descriptor will evolve, depending on what role you are going for.

Buchanan advises you to tailor your narrative to the audience. 'When you understand who you're talking to, and what matters to them in terms of culture and values, you can reflect that in the stories you tell,' she says. 'When people can see the alignment of their organisation with who you are and how you could integrate that, it gives them confidence, and it makes them feel comfortable that there would be a cultural connection.'

But what happens if you've had a blip or lull in your career due to something like a redundancy, illness, caregiving or writing a book? Do you cover that up or explain the gap in your resume? If possible, Buchanan recommends drawing on that experience and the skills you learned and bringing them to this new role. If you stayed home looking after your children or elderly parent for five years, say it. Don't apologise. Be brief and to the point.

'Unfortunately, when we're uncomfortable with something or don't know how to address it, we ramble on, drawing more attention to it,' Buchanan says. 'Be concise, be relevant and be selective about what you include. If you don't think it's going to contribute to the conversation, leave it out. There are lots of times I don't talk about my work at a digital startup because it might not be relevant to the conversation we're having.'

Emphasise your personal growth and learning

If you've had challenges in your career, use them as an illustration of what they've taught you. Highlight professional development or what stimulated you to take another path, such as further study, a PhD or an MBA.

You might say, 'I reached a point where I felt there was a ceiling in my workplace. There were no more growth opportunities unless I got another academic credential, or I felt I needed to sit on this organisation's board to give me exposure to how decisions were made, which I then brought back into my corporate career.'

The opportunity to talk about personal growth can be a way to highlight your ambitions and self-starter attitude. 'I didn't have the right expertise to progress there, or I noticed the industry was changing with AI, so I reappraised my direction and goals.'

How much personal detail should you divulge?

When it comes to showing your personality in an interview or career, be strategic about how much of your private life you reveal and what you wish to keep private. Some people are comfortable being an 'open book', and in the era of social media and the working-from-home Zoom meeting, the boundaries between the professional and personal have definitely blurred. But rather than thinking about what you feel comfortable sharing, assess what's relevant or appropriate for your audience.

Most people prefer not to post anything personal on LinkedIn. However, your 'brand' may be about transparency, and you might disclose your struggles and triumphs for good reason. Ricky Kremer is the team lead at the National Centre of Excellence in Intellectual Disability Health. His job is to talk publicly about his experiences as a person with an intellectual disability when visiting a doctor or other health practitioners. His mission is to close the health gap between those with an intellectual disability and the general population. His YouTube talks about being bullied as a child and dismissed by doctors will break your heart but also wake you up to his plight and that of others like him.

Before you speak in the workplace or post on a professional platform, ask yourself: Why are you revealing this information? To what end? How will it help others or reflect on you? How will it help or hinder your career or cause?

What's your superpower?

This is another question that can throw candidates. It sounds like the interviewer expects you to tame dragons or fly through walls; what they're really asking is what comes naturally to you? Often, this is a skill you wouldn't expect to monetise. You might have the ability to listen to a song a few times and then strum it on the guitar or buy a frumpy op shop frock and remodel it into a stylish outfit. Think about something you do so easily and naturally that it doesn't seem like work.

One of my friends studied science in Toronto and then used her talent at analysing statistics to work in advertising in Canada and Australia. Even now, semi-retired, she has started a side hustle as a bookkeeper because she simply 'likes numbers'. It's easy and relaxing for her to 'play with figures'.

Even if you're not directly asked, offer up your skill. It's not boastful; it could benefit someone or an entire organisation. You never know where it could lead.

Shulin Lee is the founder of Aslant Legal, a Singapore-based legal recruitment company. She has interviewed hundreds of high performers and claims that what makes them stand out is that they never miss an opportunity to highlight their expertise, skills and the lessons they've learned along the way. In addition, they never give generic answers.

According to Lee, these are the eight make-or-break responses to typical job interview questions:

1. 'Tell me about yourself.'
    ✗ Rambling life story.
    ✓ 'I got into [field] because [reason]. Each role sharpened my expertise in [area], and I'm ready to contribute here.'

2. 'Why do you want to work here?'
    ✗ 'I love your company!'
    ✓ 'You're leading in [specific innovation], and I'm keen to bring my [skills] to make that happen.'

3. 'Why are you leaving your current job?'
    ✗ Trashing your boss/company.
    ✓ 'I've grown as much as I can there. I'm ready for bigger challenges. Your company is the next step.'

4. 'Tell me about a time you failed.'
    ✗ 'I work too hard.'

✓ 'I misjudged [situation], made [mistake], learned [lesson] and now apply [strategy] to avoid it.'

5. 'What's your biggest career win?'
   ✗ 'I worked hard and it turned out well.'
   ✓ 'I identified [gap], implemented [solution] and improved [metric] by [action] – now that's best practice.'

6. 'How do you handle conflict?'
   ✗ 'I avoid it.'
   ✓ 'I focus on root causes. I recently resolved a team conflict by fixing a broken process.'

7. 'What sets you apart from other candidates?'
   ✗ 'I'm hardworking.'
   ✓ 'With [skillset], I drove [result] at [company]. I'll apply the same approach to your [department].'

8. 'What are your salary expectations?'
   ✗ Giving a number too soon.
   ✓ 'I'd love to understand the role's scope first. What range do you have in mind?'

It's crucial to rehearse your answers before any interview with a reliable friend, colleague or family member.

Finally, if you're just starting out and don't have the luxury of looking back on your career and drawing out the themes that make sense of it, Petra Buchanan says it's your attitude, not just your qualifications and experience, that will make you stand out in a competitive job market. How you engage with people is your winning formula. At the end of the day, we all want to work with people who are easy to get along with and who we can rely on to get the job done.

CHAPTER 4

Body language and delivery

It's not just what you say that's important; it's how you say it. As American essayist, lecturer and philosopher Ralph Waldo Emerson put it, 'Your actions speak so loud, I cannot hear what you're saying.'

Have you ever been in a restaurant in a foreign country and watched the other patrons? Even if you don't understand what they're saying, you might assume the couple laughing at the bar are hitting it off on their first date, or that the silent older couple are bored with each other, or that the four young guys in suits are negotiating a lucrative business deal.

How do we derive all this meaning without hearing the dialogue? Well, from their gestures, eye contact, facial expressions, proximity to each other, vocal tone, volume and pace. The truth is, no matter how clever we believe we are at reading body language and vocal cues, without understanding the words, we are simply using our imagination to fill in the blanks. We might have the stories completely wrong. The older couple may be sitting in companionable silence, while the guys in suits are on their way to a funeral. We are simply jumping to conclusions.

Albert Mehrabian, Emeritus Professor of Psychology at UCLA, came up with a communication model back in the

'60s that some trainers still teach today. Mehrabian claimed that 55 per cent of our message is delivered through our facial expressions and body language, 38 per cent through our tone and intonation, and only 7 per cent from our actual words. However, we know now that Mehrabian's work was misconstrued. His results were from experiments in which the words *didn't* match the speakers' expression or tone. For example, if you ask your child or partner how their day was and they say 'great' but their tone is flat and they avoid eye contact, you are unlikely to believe their words. Mehrabian's model only applies when your words and body language don't match.

Remember Barack Obama's speech about how words matter? Your words are the star attraction of your presentation, while your body language and vocal tone are notable supporting actors. Let's explore how these useful assistants can elevate your performance.

Facial expressions

There's a famous TV news clip of federal MP Bob Katter being asked by a journalist about his views on the same sex marriage vote. Bob smiles and chortles – magnanimous and mocking all at once. 'Well, people are entitled to their own sexual proclivities. I mean, let there be a thousand blossoms bloom … heh, heh, heh …' And then Katter's face darkens. His brow furrows and his voice drops to a growl, like a pantomime villain. 'But I ain't spending any time on it, because in the meantime, every three months a person is torn to pieces by a crocodile in North Queensland!' The pivot is so extreme that it takes your breath away.

Unfortunately for Bob Katter, the clip is remembered mainly for his amateur theatrics rather than his political message. Ideally, your expressions should reflect your message. If you are genuine, you won't have to 'act' the part. In your excitement about your cutting-edge research or new product offer, you'll naturally widen your eyes, raise your eyebrows and smile broadly. Conversely, if you're critical of a government policy, your tone will be sombre, your eyes and mouth will be downcast.

If you're on a panel, it can be tricky to maintain an interested or neutral facial expression while listening to the other speakers. Out of respect for their opinion, even if you don't agree with it, try not to grimace or look horrified – that will draw attention towards you and away from the speaker. Save your fire for when it's your turn to speak and rebut their claims.

Eye contact

Our eye contact, or lack of it, can be interpreted in many ways. Like a lot of spurious claims about body language, there are many exceptions to the rules depending on context, cultural norms, personality types and neurodivergence. In some cultures, looking directly at your elders is discouraged, while in Western cultures, *not* looking at your elders is regarded as disrespectful.

As far as presenting goes, there are some basic rules most

people agree on. For example, if you maintain fairly constant eye contact with your audience, you'll appear confident, friendly and trustworthy. Conversely, if you look down at your shoes, your notes or your slide deck, you may appear shy or bored.

When presenting to a small group of four or five, make eye contact with each member, perhaps giving a smidge more attention to the key decision-maker. Ideally, eye contact should be random, not rhythmic. This means you don't stare at each person from left to right and then start again in the same pattern – that looks a little spooky. Instead, look at each person randomly, remembering to include those on the outer edges.

Speaking in an auditorium

This can be a tricky scenario, especially if the only lights are on you and you can't see the audience in the dark. It requires a little magical thinking. Begin by anchoring yourself by looking at the illuminated faces in the front row, then imagine rows of giant triangles equally spaced throughout the audience. Depending on the audience size, each triangle might represent 10–20 people. Look into the centre of each imaginary triangle. To the audience members, it will feel as if you are looking directly at them. Continue sharing your eye contact with the triangles, randomly, not rhythmically, throughout your presentation. Don't forget to include the people on the sides, up the back and right down at the front. The aim is to make all audience members feel included and valued.

Speaking on a panel

You're one of four panellists and a moderator is standing at the lectern. One of the panellists is on a roll and the moderator is struggling to turn them off. Rather than looking intently at your sweaty notes or staring off into the middle distance, divide your eye contact between the current speaker, the moderator and the audience. You can take a sneaky glance at your notes to check a statistic before you speak, but don't linger there. Watch how breakfast TV hosts do it when there are several people on the couch, and they do their 'jokey bit' between the news and the sports report. They divide their eye contact between the camera (the audience) and the speaker.

Gestures

In days gone by, public speaking trainers would advise presenters to clasp their hands behind their backs, pin them to their sides or pitch a tent with their fingers as if giving a sermon. Fortunately, we've thrown out those old rules. Using your hands to speak is as natural as breathing. Even blind presenters gesture. A study by Georgia State University involving congenitally blind participants – one group English-speaking and the other Turkish-speaking – showed that their gestures were influenced by the grammar and syntax of their respective languages, rather than from any visual learning.

Some people use their hands more than others, but appropriate gestures are a way to underpin what you're saying and help your audience better understand your message. The key tip is that your gestures should match what you're saying and not contradict it; otherwise, you may confuse your audience.

For example, if I said, 'We've just got a little problem to discuss here,' and I held my arms out as if I were embracing a large beach ball, or I said, 'You'll be getting a big salary bonus this year,' and my fingers were pinched around an imaginary matchbox, you'd be more likely to believe my visual clues rather than my words. Similarly, if you're in a cafe and hold up two fingers and say, 'Three coffees, please,' the waiter will probably bring you two coffees or ask you to repeat your order. Don't baffle your audience. Use your gestures to subtly illustrate your story, but without doing an interpretative dance routine.

According to some human behaviouralists, when we first meet someone, we like to see them smile and show their open palms. In early human society, an open palm was believed to demonstrate that the stranger wasn't holding a rock or sharp instrument. Today's wave and handshake also signal you're a friend, not a foe. Therefore, if you tuck your hands behind your back or stuff them in your pockets, we may worry you're hiding something – literally. Crossing your arms could be a sign you're cold, or it could be interpreted as a defensive or resistant attitude.

A yoga teacher once said in my class, 'Open armpits mean an open mind.' Human behaviouralists tend to agree. Be as open with your gestures as possible, which means having some space between your arms and the sides of your body.

Body language expert and author Vanessa Van Edwards claims that if you want to exude competence and warmth, your gestures should be expansive rather than restrictive and close to your body. Her research team has painstakingly counted the number of gestures in the most popular TED talks. In a LinkedIn article, Van Edwards explains that the frequently viewed speakers gestured more than 450 times, while the presenters of the least-watched TED talks displayed only half that number.

Posture and movement

Your posture, like your gestures, should also be confident, open and welcoming. If you shuffle into a meeting or onto a stage, round-shouldered and slumped, people may think you're unwell or indifferent. Instead, put your shoulders back, hold your head high and keep your spine erect. Sometimes, nerves make us pace up and down the stage like a caged tiger at the zoo. When you stand on the podium, plant your feet hip-distance apart and be still. Don't cross your legs, as if you need to pee, or pin your arms tightly to your sides while tapping your feet nervously. If you are going to move in your presentation, do it deliberately rather than absent-mindedly. Van Edwards says she likes to start her presentation in the centre of the stage with a strong opening statement, then she'll walk to the left of the stage and deliver her scientific research and statistics and then move to the right of the stage to tell a personal story or anecdote. She'll repeat this process throughout her presentation. This helps the audience visualise the story arc or structure of her talk.

Similarly, you can bring to life the 'point, past, present, future, point' structure by standing centre stage for your first point, then move to the left to paint the picture of the past, then walk further right for the present-day situation, and then step to the far right of the stage to reveal your vision for the future. Finally, return to centre stage for the closing statement. You might think this choreography seems a little contrived, but if you can pull it off to appear natural, it can be a powerful technique. Ask someone to film you while you rehearse. Watching yourself can help identify areas for improvement in your body language, gestures and facial expressions.

Use of palm cards or notes

If you prefer to use palm cards or notes when giving a presentation, here are some guidelines to ensure you still maintain as much eye contact as possible with the audience:

- Use five cards (12.7 x 7.6 cm or 3 x 5 inch) and write on one side only.
- Use one card for the introduction.
- Use one card for each of the three main points, key statistics or examples.
- Use one card for the conclusion.
- Hold the card by its corner in your non-dominant hand.
- Gesture with your other hand, swapping occasionally.
- Use a large font, with key words only – don't write your entire speech on them.

Here are some of my pet peeves around using notes while presenting:

- Don't read notes from your phone. Yes, I realise this is a generational thing, but it looks like you're checking your social media or emails and not focusing on your audience.
- Avoid reading out each PowerPoint slide. Your audience can read too, and faster than you can say it out loud. Your slides should contain minimal text.
- Don't wave around the slide clicker or whiteboard marker for the entire presentation. It's distracting and constrains your natural hand gestures. Consider asking an assistant to operate your slide deck.

If you're using an autocue that's operated by someone else, make sure you rehearse with them before your presentation. The autocue operator will adjust the speed of the script to your reading pace. A professional operator will position the lines you're reading in the centre of the camera or screen so the audience perceives only minimal eye movement and can't tell you're reading. Wear your glasses if you need them or ask the operator to increase the font size. Avoid squinting at the script – that's a dead giveaway that you're reading. If you've written the script yourself, it should be conversational. Underline or italicise words in the script you want to emphasise and spell out difficult pronunciations.

Wear what suits you

In March 2025, President Volodymyr Zelenskyy met with President Trump and Vice President Vance at the Oval Office in a bid to negotiate peace in Ukraine. After enduring Trump's and Vance's verbal slings and arrows, the first question from the press gallery was: 'Why aren't you wearing a suit?'

Brian Glenn, a reporter for the conservative cable network *Real America's Voice*, called out, 'You're at the highest level in this country's office, and you refuse to wear a suit.' He continued: 'A lot of Americans have a problem with you not respecting the dignity of this office.' Zelenskyy claimed he wore military-style shirts and trousers in solidarity with his soldiers and fellow citizens under attack. He says he'll wear a suit when there's peace.

So, does it really matter what we wear publicly, and what message do our clothes, hair and shoes send to our audience? According to two style experts I interviewed, our professional attire is important, especially if we're being interviewed on camera, speaking on an industry panel or giving a presentation. Samantha Theron, Global Senior Visual Merchandising Manager for RM Williams, says, 'It takes one tenth of a second to make a judgement about someone. We all do it, whether we like it or not.'

'When you make an effort with your appearance, it shows how much effort you put into everything,' Theron continues. 'Combed hair, ironed clothes, shined shoes signal you are capable and pay attention to detail.'

Lia Tsimos, the founder and designer of fashion label MOSS & SPY, says first impressions are everything. 'I have already judged you before you speak.' Ouch. That seems a little harsh, but possibly true. She advises people to be true to their own style by asking themselves:

- Where am I going?
- Who is my audience?
- What do I want people to think about me?
- Does my clothing say I am innovative and creative or conservative and dull?

Both stylists recommend revealing your personality by adding a touch of flair to a well-tailored suit, such as a patterned shirt, colourful scarf or tie or a tasteful piece of jewellery.

Other recommendations include wearing a style and colour that complements your body shape and skin colour. Avoid wearing anything too distracting, especially on an online presentation, such as jangly jewellery, pin stripes or complicated patterns. Don't wear the same colour as your background or you'll disappear. If you're on a stage, consider whether you'll be sitting or standing and whether your outfit will be suitable. Make sure you feel comfortable and that your clothes reflect your brand, personality and message.

There are, of course, eccentric public figures who break the mould exceptionally well. Their maverick look makes them memorable and reflects their personal brand. Iris Apfel, a flamboyant New York interior designer who died in 2024 at the age of 102, wore eye-popping outfits, a swag of costume jewellery and her trademark oversized glasses. Gina Chick, author and winner of the SBS *Alone* series, doesn't wear shoes – not even on the red carpet to a premiere. She says going barefoot connects her to nature.

There's no doubt women bear the brunt of criticism from the style police. In an experiment, Channel Nine's *Today* host Karl Stefanovic wore the same blue suit every morning on air for a year, and no one seemed to notice. Meanwhile, his then co-host Lisa Wilkinson received regular and sometimes savage criticism about her hair, clothes and makeup. In an interview with the *Sydney Morning Herald*, Stefanovic said, 'Women are judged much more harshly and keenly for what they do, what they say and what they wear.'

Fortunately, the rules around women's fashion are not as rigid as they once were. Former model and founder of Australia's first deportment school, June Dally-Watkins, gave her female students this advice: 'Don't wear dark underpants under light-coloured dresses and never let your bra strap show when you're wearing a sleeveless top.' June also discouraged plunging necklines. 'You want people looking at your smile, not your weapons of mass distraction,' she said.

It's likely June would have advised President Zelenskyy to comply with the Oval Office dress code, although plenty admire his non-conformity. After all, you rarely see a TED talk speaker in a jacket and tie these days. The bottom line is this: be intentional about the message you want to send and wear what suits you.

Voice

Your voice conveys so many messages beyond the actual words you use. You want your delivery to be well paced so you're engaging while making it easy for your audience to follow your logic. If you speak too fast, you'll sound flustered or nervous and people might miss what you're saying. Then again, when you speak too slowly, you'll bore people to tears.

Aim for the 'Goldilocks and the Three Bears' formula – not too fast, not too slow, but just right.

The same principle applies to volume. Avoid shouting at everybody. That's terrifying and off-putting, like a red-faced soccer coach screaming at the under-12s team. However, you don't want to speak too softly, either, because then you'll sound uncertain and lack authority. Although, when we intentionally lower our voice at key points, we invite people to listen intently, as if we're sharing a juicy secret they don't want to miss.

Equally as important are the key words you choose to emphasise to convey meaning. Here's a quick exercise. Say this sentence out loud – six times. Each time you say it, emphasise the italicised word. Go on, ham it up:

I didn't say he stole the money.
I *didn't* say he stole the money.
I didn't *say* he stole the money.
I didn't say *he* stole the money.
I didn't say he *stole* the money.
I didn't say he stole the *money*.

Depending on which word you stress, you change the story's meaning. Be deliberate about which words, statistics or phrases you highlight. It can be useful to emphasise statistics, because they're harder for most people to grasp the first time they hear them.

What about your tone and intonation? Are you speaking enthusiastically and positively? Or are you speaking in a serious, sombre tone? Of course, it will depend on the subject.

You won't be speaking in a happy voice if there's been a terrible accident.

There also needs to be variety in your pace, volume, emphasis, tone and intonation. If you speak in a monotone, you'll sound like a train rumbling rhythmically over the tracks, over and over, rocking your audience to sleep.

Your tone and intonation are also connected to your vocal register. Most adults limit themselves to a narrow band of their potential vocal range. We've lost the impressive wail we had as babies – thank goodness – although sometimes it comes out when we're cheering for our football team or singing karaoke. You probably have a far greater range than you normally use.

Most leaders tend to command with deeper, warmer voices. But beware. Don't try to make your voice too low or you may end up with vocal fry and damage your vocal cords. Some young women deliberately use vocal fry because they believe a husky voice sounds cool and sexy. If you're a trained singer, a dash of fry can add a certain desirable timbre to your song, but using it all the time, in your day-to-day speaking voice, is like sunbaking your vocal cords. Instead, speak louder and use your full breath to vibrate your vocal cords freely.

The accidental question inflection

Have you ever heard a statement that sounds like a question? Avoid ending your sentences with an upward inflection; it undermines your authority. Some people even use the so-called accidental question inflection when they say their names. 'Hello, I'm Theresa Miller?' Then they wonder why they can't close a deal when, at the end of their business pitch, they say,

'This service will cost you $5000?' It sounds like you're asking permission instead of stating a fact.

The upward inflection can be common among younger people, and especially Australian girls and women. The accidental question inflection makes the speaker appear unsure, and it can make the listener feel nervous too. Imagine if your surgeon said, 'I'm going to operate now on your right knee?' You'd be thinking, 'Gosh, I'd better stay awake and make sure they don't cut open the left one.'

Finish your statements with a definite downward inflection to sound assured, authoritative and competent. You can, of course, go to a voice coach if you feel it would benefit you. There are also speech pathologists who can help.

In the meantime, breathing correctly will help enormously. Rather than breathing through your nose or your throat, breathe from your chest and your abdomen. That gives you a deeper register, so you sound more convincing. It can help calm you down too.

Try these warm-up exercises before a presentation. Raise your arms, take a deep breath and exhale slowly to the count of four. Do that three times. Next, practise warming up with some tongue trills. There are two types: one in which you keep your lips still while fluttering your tongue on the out breath, and the other in which your lips and tongue vibrate together, such as 'brrrrrrr'. Another effective vocal warm-up to loosen your lips, tongue and jaw is to make the sound 'ba, ba, ba' on an easy out breath. Some people swear by tongue twisters to improve their articulation and focus. Or you could simply practise your key points out loud.

The power of the pause

Another powerful tool in public speaking is the pause. Often, when we're buying time to think, we 'um' and 'er', but that just muddies the message. It's far more effective to pause to allow your audience to digest what you've said. This gives you a breather and flags that you're moving on to a new point.

Since 1924, Toastmasters have held regular meetings around the world to help people become better communicators and leaders. I visited my local club recently and was surprised to see that someone sits at the back of the room and counts all the 'ums' and 'ers' during each presentation. The counter reports the grand total to the group at the end of the evening. I'm not sure if that helps or hinders people. It can be a little daunting. But what Toastmasters does well is give presenters feedback notes on their talk, and that is vital for ongoing improvement.

Use feedback to improve your performance

When I run presenting workshops, we film each participant at least once, and then play it back so they can observe their performance. Often, they're pleasantly surprised to see they don't look as nervous as they feel.

Almost always, they discover something they do unconsciously, such as jiggling their leg, fiddling with their clothes or overusing a particular word or phrase. The exercise is not designed to make them feel self-conscious; rather, it's to reveal what they do well and what they might consider improving next time.

Below is a typical feedback report I send participants after a workshop. This was for a marketing professional preparing to pitch a new product range.

Strengths
- Good opener with an intriguing question
- Knowledgeable and personable
- Clear and confident speech
- Appeared authoritative and credible
- Plain English – minimal jargon
- Slides were relevant and added interest rather than distraction
- Gave an interesting potted history of China's consumer market in the past 40 years
- Connected points well with a logical structure and bridging phrase
- Clear summary at the end
- Great storytelling techniques – 'As we're sitting here today, a quiet storm is taking over …'

For next time
- Use the pause more for dramatic effect, especially after revealing the product
- Slow down – you are delivering a lot of new information fast, which can be hard for the audience to digest
- Have a slide with key statistics to underpin your points
- Stand with both feet planted firmly on the ground – hip-distance apart, rather than jiggling on one leg

- Release your hands and allow them to express and underpin your points
- Use 'you' rather than 'I' to engage the audience
- Use more light and shade in your voice to draw us into the story
- Give us concrete examples rather than abstract concepts
- What's in it for the audience (e.g. how will it benefit them)?
- Avoid looking back at the screen to read – it breaks eye contact
- Avoid starting every sentence with 'So'
- Correct distracting typos in the slide
- End with a stronger call to action, specific and dated (e.g. what do you want the audience to do with the information you have just shared with them?)

General comments

You are a natural storyteller and know how to hook your audience. In the second presentation, your pause was more effective, and you used compelling phrases such as 'This is not child's play; this is big business.'

The second pitch was better structured, and the argument was more persuasive. With practice, you will elevate your presentation skills to the next level.

Well done.

If you don't have the luxury of a professional presentation coach, you can always record your rehearsal and play it back. Try watching your video with the volume down. What is your body language communicating? Next, listen to the audio without looking at the vision. What message is your voice conveying? Try not to be too harsh on yourself by picking on every little flaw. Focus on your strengths and specific ideas for next time.

You could even ask a couple of dependable colleagues and friends to give you some constructive feedback. The following list of feedback points is a useful guide:

- first impression
- audience engagement
- choice of language
- structure
- gestures and body language
- eye contact
- voice – pace, tone, emphasis
- use of the stage
- use of notes
- call to action.

Presenting, like any new skill, takes practice. If you only do it once a year or once in a decade, it's difficult to build on your successes and refine your techniques. If you're serious about becoming an accomplished public speaker, take any opportunity you can to present and pitch. Learn from your mistakes. Watch great presenters and analyse what they do well. Mastering public speaking is an investment in your ability to lead, persuade, connect and influence. It's a skill for life.

CHAPTER 5

How to be a confident media spokesperson

Many organisations miss golden opportunities to tell their 'good news' stories because they avoid the media. However, if you understand what a journalist is looking for in a news story, you can use the media to boost your visibility and influence.

Stephen Watson, a communications strategist, coaches business and political leaders on how to present and conduct interviews with journalists. He recommends being strategic about which interviews you agree to. 'It's not about celebrity. It's not just about creating noise. I encourage people to be very calculated, and that means saying no to some media interviews. It's clearly got to be within your interests.'

There's no doubt a media interview can be daunting. Despite having been a TV and radio journalist for 20 years and a media trainer and lecturer for almost another 20, I have also been misquoted in the media. If you're from a large organisation, you may be lucky enough to have PR and communications professionals to vet media enquiries, but if it's just you, you'll need to decide whether the interview is an opportunity or a trap.

Before you agree to an interview, ask the journalist a series of questions. Where are you from? Who is your audience? Is this a news story or a feature? If the interview is for TV or radio, will it be a live interview or pre-recorded? When will the story go to air/be published? What angle are you taking? Who else have you or will you be interviewing? Make sure you have a clear agenda. It's important to remember you are a spokesperson, not simply someone who answers questions.

Watson views a media interview as a two-way contract. 'You're not doing yourself any favours or honouring your side of the contract if you simply sit there and get pummelled with a series of questions and don't use the opportunity to advance your own thinking, insights, points or whatever it is that you want to do. There's an elegant dance in achieving both agendas.'

Don't be afraid to negotiate the time and place of the interview to suit both of you. You can position a camera crew in front of your logo or products. Keep in mind that TV interviews need much more time than radio or print/online interviews. A camera crew will need a quiet place to set up for the interview and then film B-roll to cover the introduction to set the scene and introduce you. This is usually when the news producer or reporter instructs you to type on your computer, walk down the street or enter the lift of your building. If you're creative, you'll set up a more eye-catching scene that relates to what you're talking about. Take the crew into the lab where you're working or give them some stunning drone footage of the property or vineyard you're representing. No matter how interesting your topic is, TV reporters will be reluctant to cover your story if there are no pictures to go along with it.

Put yourself in the shoes of a reporter or producer. Many journalists see themselves as watchdogs acting in the public's interest. Their investigations help hold the government and companies to account. To do their jobs well, they need credible sources and facts, quotes or soundbites, as well as vision and audio for TV and radio.

In commercial media, reporters like to beat their competitors to a story to gain an exclusive. They must meet tight deadlines and, like in any competitive industry, they're often seeking the approval of their boss (chief of staff, executive producer) as well as their peers.

It's also helpful to remember that journalists need you more than you need them. They need a subject matter expert to give their story credibility. An article without quotes from an expert is just an opinion piece. Handled well, an interview with the media can:

- raise your organisation's visibility and your own career profile
- celebrate your and your team's hard work
- inform and educate the public and your stakeholders
- attract funding, clients and staff
- influence policymakers
- debunk myths
- position you as an industry thought leader
- inspire the next generation.

Underlining all this is your objective to promote and protect your professional reputation. Now more than ever, we need subject matter experts to communicate clearly and truthfully so we can help stamp out misinformation. Many investigative journalists are under fire. The British docudrama

2073 features interviews with several investigative journalists who have risked their livelihoods to hold power to account, including *The Guardian* journalist Carole Cadwalladr, who uncovered the Facebook Cambridge Analytica scandal; Maria Ressa, the award-winning journalist of *Rappler* who has been jailed multiple times for exposing corruption in the Philippines; and Indian columnist Rana Ayyub, whose bank accounts were frozen after she alleged Narendra Modi's government was behind attacks on Indian Muslims. Cadwalladr urges us to protect journalists' rights to report freely without fear of censorship and legal battles. 'You'll miss facts when they're gone,' she says.

Despite the challenges in today's media landscape, there are reasons to be hopeful. With so many specialist podcasts, trade magazines, Substack contributors and content platforms, there are opportunities for subject matter experts like you to combat fake news and misinformation with evidence, facts and experience. If you want to proactively pitch a story to a specialist podcast or media outlet, you need to understand what a journalist or content producer is looking for. There's an old saying, 'To catch a thief, think like a thief.' The same goes for capturing the attention of a journalist by knowing what makes news.

Town criers to TikTok – how we consume news

In Stephen Lamble's book *News As It Happens*, he reminds us that humans have been sharing news since cave dwellers swapped stories around the campfire. Some of the hunting tales depicted on cave walls could be considered the world's first news images. The ancient Greeks and Romans exchanged news stories in the marketplace. While people from the forests of West Africa, Asia and the Amazon beat giant drums to send long-distance headlines, wandering minstrels in medieval Europe rang bells, and town criers called out to inform villagers of the latest royal proclamations.

When we look back at what our ancestors went through to find out what was happening in their world, and even the journalists who have risked their lives to report on wars, injustice and corruption, it seems surreal that we have up-to-the-minute news at our fingertips around the clock. We wake up in the morning, roll over and open our phones to see images of earthquakes in Myanmar and videos of verbal ripostes between pop stars and billionaires. While our ancestors had to wait months for a travelling merchant (an early influencer) to come to their village with news from the city, we have access to immediate accounts of events in countries we've never visited and about people we've never met. The trickle of news is now a virtual tsunami.

How we access news has never been so varied, and our preferences are drawn along the generational divide. According to the Australian Communications and Media Authority, free-to-air TV and news websites are still Australia's most popular news platforms, while 46 per cent of younger Australians aged 18 to 34 prefer social media as their primary news source. Only around 15 per cent of the population had read a printed newspaper in the week of the survey. Even politicians can't ignore social media's influence on young people's opinions. In a bid for the Gen Z vote, a dozen digital influencers were invited to the 2025 budget lock-up in Parliament House for the first time and given access to one-on-one interviews with the prime minister, treasurer and opposition leader to discuss the budget and upcoming election.

The credibility crisis

The ever-increasing quantity and decreasing quality of news have fuelled mistrust in the media. According to the annual Edelman Trust Barometer, which surveys the public's view of governments, institutions, business and the media, 69 per cent of Australians believe the media deceives us in a bid to push their ideologies and grow their audiences.

PR strategist Stephen Watson says the age of deference has vanished, meaning that everyone is fair game. He believes there is no such thing as 'accidental communication' now. 'It's a very unforgiving world. And whether it's a ten-second clip on social media or an in-depth interview on traditional media, communication skills really do matter.'

When marketing agencies talk about 'brand equity' and the rise and fall of share prices, they are really talking about old-fashioned trust and reputation, which is intrinsically linked to a leader's ability to invoke trust and empathy.

'It goes to the heart of their ability to persuade and to shape audiences' minds,' Watson says. 'This is very precious, and it needs to be nurtured, especially at a time when freedom of speech and democratic values are under attack.'

While Southeast Queensland waited for Cyclone Alfred to cross the coast in March 2025, residents were bombarded with a barrage of phone updates from media outlets, local government, the Bureau of Meteorology (BoM), independent weather accounts and influencers. Some online posts catastrophised events with fake videos, while others downplayed warnings. When it comes to deciding whether to close the airport, 'strongly held opinions' are no substitute for hard facts and evidence from trained meteorologists at the BoM.

Digital strategist Erinn Swan, who calls southeast Queensland home, wrote an opinion piece in the *Brisbane Times* and the *Sydney Morning Herald* of her experience of waiting for Alfred. Faced with a confusing deluge of opinion, misinformation and disinformation, she said many residents tuned out of the news when they should have stayed informed for their safety. Alarm and outrage fuel algorithms and attract eyeballs to social media accounts. Influencers don't need to abide by the journalist's code of ethics, nor do they have an obligation to check the facts.

'The lack of hierarchy in information isn't just frustrating – it's dangerous,' Swan wrote. 'We're bombarded every second with a mix of fact, fiction, misinformation, disinformation, AI-generated nonsense and complete bollocks – all in equal measure … we need to elevate informed voices in an emergency, not compete with them.'

While fake news has always been around, social media has turbo-charged it. Bad agents are using social media to create bogus stories that look like bona fide news stories, especially during an election campaign.

Megan Davis, a renowned constitutional and human rights lawyer, partly blames the defeat of the referendum on the Indigenous voice to parliament on a coordinated campaign of disinformation and untruths. Speaking on a panel at UNSW on misinformation and the media, Davis said that the Voice referendum was Australia's first experience of a US-style disinformation campaign.

'Advance [a right-wing lobby group] was really clever. They started early and got their money outside the statutory declaration period,' Davis said. 'Advance produced what looked like a neutral news site on referendum news before it was in the consciousness of most Australians, and that had a huge influence on people's sentiments.' Davis also blames journalists for not fact-checking and for permitting Advance's talking points on TikTok to set the news agenda each day. Post-analysis of the campaign unearthed thousands of spam accounts linked to the Chinese Communist Party used to flood social media with negative information.

Professor Davis says we may all have been caught on the hop during the referendum, but we'll be better armed to combat misinformation in the future. Or will we?

While there's much commentary about how digital news feeds separate us into silos and lead to a divisive and polarised society, at its best, the news can bring us together. When the Matildas, Australia's national women's football team, win, every media outlet in the country unanimously celebrates with headlines of praise. But it doesn't have to be just sport that unites us. A free and uncensored news media underpins a democracy and is worth upholding.

And there is more good news. Among the newcomers

is an emerging breed of storytellers with noble intentions. Australian podcast and newsletter *The Squiz* was launched in 2017 to be a 'shortcut to being informed'. Founder Claire Kimball identified a need to tell people about the top news stories each day without overwhelming them. *The Squiz* presents news without an agenda, opinion or assumption that you understand the backstory to a complex issue. The podcast is usually under ten minutes long and appeals to busy people and the growing number of news-avoiders, the majority of whom are young women.

I subscribed to *The Squiz* back when it was a simple email newsletter. I encouraged my journalism students to subscribe as well, and each week we played the Squiz Quiz to test if they'd been paying attention. *The Squiz* team has grown considerably since then, and they have a kids' version called *Newshounds*, which runs media literacy programs in primary schools. *Newshounds* is lobbying the government to fund the program in all Australian schools, arguing that media-literate kids will make better-informed voters. *The Squiz* recently produced a podcast about media literacy education in Finland and Estonia, where children are taught from day one to sort fact from fiction. Sharing borders with Russia, the Finns and Estonians view misinformation and propaganda as existential threats to their democracy.

What makes the news?

There are potentially millions of news yarns out there, and yet every day we are fed a similar diet of news content through our social feeds and traditional media. So, what makes a story newsworthy and how can you use this knowledge to become a quotable spokesperson and pitch your own story to a journalist?

New, topical and trending

If you want to grab media attention, use a news event as a hook to promote your topic or campaign. This is known as 'newsjacking', where an organisation strategically piggybacks on a trending topic to insert their brand or campaign into the news cycle. Unfortunately, it's gained a negative reputation following some tone-deaf PR marketing pranks, but if used sensitively, this can be a legitimate way to highlight an issue that may otherwise fly under the radar.

YFS Ltd (formerly Youth and Family Services) is a not-for-profit organisation that provides support and advocates for vulnerable groups in Logan, west of Brisbane. The number of people sleeping rough each night in Logan has grown from 95 people to around 350 in the past five years, and that doesn't include the hidden homeless rate of people couch surfing, squatting or living in overcrowded digs. The average rent has almost doubled during that period, while Centrelink payments have remained static. Consequently, many Centrelink recipients are priced out of the rental market.

In the lead-up to the federal budget, there was a lot of pressure on the government to address 'cost of living' pressures. Logan happened to be Treasurer Jim Chalmer's electorate. This was the perfect opportunity for YFS to pitch their CEO, Christopher John, for an interview on ABC TV

Breakfast on the eve of the budget announcement. I met with John and the rest of the YFS team the day before and we rehearsed key messages, questions and answers on camera. The next morning, John appeared on the show, nailing his key messages concisely and in plain English. He called on the government to invest in affordable housing to alleviate the crisis. It was a perfectly timed message.

Exceptional

Every journalist is on the hunt for an event that is out of the ordinary. As John Bogar, former editor of the *New York Sun*, allegedly once said: 'When a dog bites a man, that's not news; but when a man bites a dog, that's news.'

An exceptional news event is when something happens for the first time or the last time, or it's the fastest, biggest, smallest, most expensive, most popular or most unusual. For example, 'It's the wettest July on record' or 'The biggest price rise in a decade' or 'Zoo announces the birth of critically endangered red-bellied lemurs'. This last one has the wow factor because lemurs are photogenic, making them perfect for TV news and social media.

What is it about your research, product, service, event, book or campaign that makes it exceptional and out of the ordinary?

Relevance, proximity, impact

There are plenty of remarkable stories that go unreported. We tend to look at what's happening at home before we look overseas – unless it's a huge international story with local impact, such as tariffs, a war or a pandemic.

But as American marketers like to say: 'There are riches in niches.' This parochialism can be used to your advantage if you're targeting a particular audience. Don't overlook relevant trade magazines, local suburban newspapers, community radio and specialist websites and publications to pitch your story.

Karen Eck and Samantha Theron are the founders of a monthly networking event called Collabor8Women. Every month, they choose a female-led restaurant venue to host curated tables of eight designed to introduce professional women to each other in a welcoming environment.

When they announced their list of 2025 venues in advance, Eck sent a media release to *Hospitality* magazine, which has a highly engaged subscriber list. As a PR strategist, Eck says if you want to generate publicity, trade media is a good place to start. These are business-to-business publications specific to an industry. 'Trade media can be an excellent opportunity to gain valuable experience doing interviews, honing your message and building confidence, before promoting yourself and your business more widely,' Eck says.

The call-out in the media release and article was for female-led venues to jump on board this growing networking event and host the next Collabor8Women lunch or dinner. Eck also put forward a restaurant owner who'd hosted and attended more than 20 of their events as an interviewee for the story. It's far more powerful to use the testimonials of your happy clients and customers rather than tooting your own horn.

According to Eck and Theron, the media coverage paid off in spades: 'For the first time since launching in December 2021, venues are now reaching out to *us*, keen to collaborate.'

Controversy or conflict

Unfortunately, there's no shortage of examples in this category: the insurance company that won't pay out flood victims, opposing political parties debating fiscal policies, rival football teams disputing a penalty, countries embroiled in trade wars or a mining company's interests versus the environment. Like a match to dry grass, controversy and conflict spark outrage, which in turn attracts the most clicks and shares, going viral more speedily than any positive story ever will. When a small African nation successfully eradicates malaria, it barely makes a ripple in the social media sphere.

However, if you're caught up in a news controversy, you don't have to fuel the conflict in an interview. You need to acknowledge where things have gone wrong and how you're working to make them better. In the next chapter, I discuss how to deal with a media crisis in more detail.

Celebrity

Australian Psychological Society president Catriona Davis-McCabe says people turn to celebrities for information on current events because they admire them and want to have the same views as them. 'People typically like celebrities who confirm their own worldview, and this apparent alignment of beliefs can make chosen celebrities a more trusted source of information than is the case,' Davis-McCabe told ABC News.

Using a celebrity to endorse your campaign, product or event can be useful to attract news coverage. But do your homework on your chosen ambassador. If they've done or said anything in the past that contradicts your organisation's values, it can backfire disastrously.

Celebrity endorsements of referendums usually don't move the dial with voters either. When US basketball star Shaquille O'Neal was touring Australia in 2024 to promote a sports betting company, he shook hands with the prime minister and publicly vowed his support for the Voice's Yes campaign to enshrine an Indigenous voice in the constitution. Professor Matt Qvortrup from the Australian National University's College of Law says Australians were bemused and confused. Was the support of a US sports celebrity, visiting to promote gambling, really that helpful to the cause?

Human interest

Human interest stories undoubtedly get more cut-through than stories full of statistics. A photo of a house on the Central Coast partly washed away by the sea seized people's attention around the world far more effectively than dozens of environmental reports warning of the dangers of rising sea levels. According to social psychologist Elliot Aronson, 'Most people are more deeply influenced by one clear, vivid personal example rather than by an abundance of statistical data.'

When TV news airs a story on an interest rate hike, the first people interviewed are homeowners, before the reporter turns to a financial expert for an overview. Finding people with lived experience needs to be done sensitively. Toni Wren is a spokesperson for the End Child Poverty campaign and Principal Adviser to Single Mother Families Australia. She's very adept at pitching stories to journalists that not only personalise the statistics around poverty but also make links between legislation and outcomes.

When thousands of Australians around the country marched to end violence against women, Wren wrote an opinion piece that was published on ABC News Online, drawing the link between domestic violence and child poverty and calling for more government income support.

With these types of stories, journalists will usually request an interview with someone who has experienced domestic violence. 'We reach out to women who want to speak, both directly to politicians and to the media. A lot of women want to have their voice heard, but we handle a media request carefully to ensure they don't feel exploited, or they're used as poverty porn. We only work with journalists who are respectful,' Wren says.

If you become good at media interviews and pitching stories, you'll become the go-to person for journalists looking for comments in your field. Reporters and producers are always time-poor – they will simply google 'AI expert near me', and the first person who pops up is who they call. So, if you do decide to do the interview, here's my top tip: don't come up with an answer off the cuff. Be prepared.

It might look like you and the reporter are having a normal discussion, but the journalist is there to get quotes and you're there to deliver key messages about your organisation or cause. When I was promoting my first book, my publisher flew me to

Melbourne for an interview with a features writer. I discovered she was also a mother of young children. I confided in her that I was feeling under the weather and worried I had mastitis. Rookie mistake. Guess what the first paragraph of her article was about? My sore boobs. It was an embarrassing way to learn to never say anything off the record.

What makes someone good media talent?

Besides speaking clearly and concisely in plain English, it's the way you deliver your message that speaks volumes. Ideally, you want to appear confident and calm, empathetic, genuine and enthusiastic if it's appropriate.

It's rarely the topic that puts people to sleep; it's the way it's told. Inject energy into your delivery and you'll hold your audience's attention. It's even more crucial to dial up the animation in your voice when you're on the radio or speaking on the phone, because your listeners don't have the benefit of seeing your facial expressions and gestures.

When a journalist requests an interview with an expert, they expect them to be knowledgeable, friendly, helpful and available. It's no use if a journalist rings for a comment and you say, 'Sorry, I'm too busy. Call back tomorrow.' The journalist will simply find someone else, maybe even your competitor. The news waits for no one. However, you can set boundaries. For example, if a harried reporter rings you at 2 pm and says they need a comment for the 3 pm radio news bulletin, you might put them off until their next deadline at 4 pm or 5 pm. That will give you more time to prepare your response. Otherwise, if you bend to the journalist's pressure to respond immediately, it could be a case of 'act in haste, repent at leisure'.

Say to the producer or reporter, 'I'd be happy to talk to you, but I'm in a meeting/classroom/operating theatre. When is your next deadline, and what is it exactly you want to know?' Don't be afraid to ask the journalist what angle they're taking on the story and whether it's a news or feature article. Who else are they interviewing? That will give you enough information to prepare your responses and rehearse with a colleague before facing the camera or microphone.

Speak clearly and concisely

A journalist wants an interviewee who can speak clearly and concisely. In commercial TV and radio news reports, producers and presenters want sound bites that are between five and eight seconds. In print or online, journalists are looking for around 25 words for a quote. If you're lucky enough to be interviewed live on radio, you may get up to 12 minutes. But you still need to be prepared. The advantage – and disadvantage – of a live interview is that you can't be edited!

I was once interviewed on live commercial radio about an article I'd written in *The Australian* about being left-handed. It included facts and fictions about left-handers, including the disproportionate number of left-handed professional tennis players. Presumably, they catch their opponents off guard. Given that I had written the story, I assumed I didn't need to prepare for the interview. I was wrong. When the radio host asked me to list the names of famous left-handed tennis players, I had a momentary lapse of memory. Sometimes, when we're nervous, our prefrontal cortex freezes, and we can't access basic information. After I hung up, the names came flooding back – Martina Navratilova, Rafael Nadal, John McEnroe and Monica Seles. Do yourself a favour and prepare. Put sticky notes with statistics and key messages all over your desk where you can see them. Don't rely on your memory, especially on live radio.

Explain complex ideas simply

Anne Connolly is a Walkley Award–winning journalist with the ABC's investigative unit. When she's interviewing a subject matter expert, especially for television, she's always keeping the viewers' interest in mind. 'We don't want the audience to ever turn off or lose track of the story. If you're long-winded, boring, too complicated, using technical jargon, it's likely you won't be included in the program,' Connolly says.

When the answers are too lengthy, Connolly and her producer have to edit the responses to fit the script, which can be problematic for TV and audio programs. 'We want to ensure the response is still in context and it's correct, so it's not misinterpreting the speaker's meaning. But it's always difficult to cut things up. You might start with the beginning of it, cut a bit out, then take a section from the middle, cut a bit more out, and then link to the end bit. But sometimes the intonation isn't correct, so that won't work,' Connolly says.

During the research phase, she will pre-interview an expert on the phone to gauge whether they are 'good talent.' But she concedes some experts and academics can be hard to interview because they tend not to be as dynamic as somebody telling their own personal story, or an entertainer, who is used to the medium:

> We're often dealing with people who've never done TV before. I say, 'Please try to forget all the cameras around us and understand you and I are just having a conversation.' If their answers are too long, I'll give them some gentle advice. I might ask the question a different way, or I'll say, 'Is this what you mean? And would you be able to put it in those terms because it will be easier for the audience to understand?' If they can take that instruction, that's perfect. But there are a lot of people who are incapable of that, and they risk not making it into the program.

If the journalist is looking for quotes for print or online, it's easier to edit the quotes to fit while remaining truthful to the original response. Interviewees need to adapt their answers to the medium. In TV news, the reporter is up against a tight deadline and may only ask five to six questions. They're seeking a short, sharp grab. In a feature or documentary, your answers can be more expansive. There's room to explain your point of view.

Every industry has shorthand, which is useful when speaking to your peers, but it's unintelligible to someone outside your field. If I requested an interview with a newcomer to TV, imagine how they'd react if I said, 'We're going to shoot you in an MCU and then grab some noddies and B-roll. Then I'll pick a few grabs for tonight's promo.' The problem with jargon is that it creates a barrier between you and the listener. They'll either switch off or misinterpret your meaning. The rule of thumb is to use language understandable to a 14-year-old.

You certainly don't want to use jargon when speaking to a young, inexperienced reporter who may be too embarrassed to ask for clarification.

As a 20-year-old cadet TV journalist, I reported on a press conference in South Australia in which the attorney general announced new legislation about how children would give evidence in the family court. He said they'd give evidence '*in camera*'. In my naivety, I thought that meant children's evidence would be televised. I asked the attorney general if Channel Nine could have access to the footage. I can still recall the sniggers from the other journalists. The attorney general said gently, 'Ah, *in camera* is a legal term for *in private.*' Something I've never forgotten. For journalists, the moral of the story is that it's wiser to seek clarification, even if it means losing face, rather than misreporting the story. The lesson for spokespeople is that not everyone has studied Latin or has a law degree. Simply explain a technical phrase to avoid being misquoted.

Tech industry columnist David Pogue sums up his frustration with terminology after years of interviewing IT experts. 'I cannot stand jargon,' Pogue says. 'It exists merely to puff up the speaker at the expense of the audience. It drives me crazy.'

If you're feeling smug at this stage, thinking you communicate more plainly than scientists, lawyers or IT geeks, I can guarantee that if you're an expert, you use some sort of in-house lingo. Even well-meaning social workers sometimes lapse into bureaucratic terms such as 'stakeholders', 'self-advocacy', 'co-locate', 'recovery elements', 'deliver outcomes' and 'building capacity'. This can be confusing not only for their clients but the general public as well.

I once interviewed a police officer who was seeking eyewitnesses to a crime. He said on camera: 'A young, male Caucasian was seen decamping from the scene in a north-westerly direction after the unlawful use of a vehicle.' This is how police officers are trained to write their incident reports, but this type of jargon doesn't cut through when encouraging viewers to call Crime Stoppers. Stick to plain English.

However, one of the most impressive speakers in Australia's public service today is Australian Federal Police Commissioner Reece Kershaw. This is a direct quote from his address to the National Press Club following Elon Musk's refusal to remove graphic content from X's platform in 2024: 'Some of our children and other vulnerable people are being bewitched online by a cauldron of extremist poison on the open and dark web. And that's one serious problem. The other is that the very nature of social media allows that extremist poison to spray across the globe almost instantaneously.'

Kershaw doesn't mince his words. He doesn't use any police or tech jargon. He speaks in plain English and employs highly visual imagery. You can almost see and smell the evil brew bubbling in a blackened iron pot. This evocative language is designed to elicit a visceral response. These are not neutral words, and it's possible that, as a professional, you might not be comfortable with that, but it's hard to deny that this colourful expression cuts through and makes us take notice. If your message is important, it's worth pulling out all stops to get the right attention.

Speak to express, not to impress

Many professionals and experts have studied long and hard to acquire their degrees and qualifications, so they certainly don't want to 'dumb down' their language in case it makes them sound less credible to their peers. But here's the rub: when you are speaking to a journalist, you are not speaking to your peers; you are speaking to the public, some of whom will have more qualifications than you, and others who will have limited English and education. Use words everyone can understand.

One of the world's most famous orators was Britain's wartime prime minister Winston Churchill. He said, 'I like short words.' Churchill used plain English to great effect. Britons were weary after World War I and the Depression. Churchill's stirring speeches roused them to their feet to defend their island home from a Nazi invasion.

In a radio broadcast, Churchill said: 'We shall defend our island, whatever the cost may be. We shall fight on the beaches, we shall fight on the landing-grounds, we shall fight in the fields and in the streets, we shall fight in the hills. We shall never surrender!'

Such is the power of short words. Note: he also used the rule of three and repetition. The fate of the British Isles may have been very different if Churchill had said, 'We will seek to interdict vessels which travel here for invalid purposes,' which is what former prime minister Kevin Rudd said in a TV interview about Australia's border control operations.

Yet the war on jargon continues today. We are drowning under a deluge of corporate, political and marketing gobbledy-gook that casts a veil of miscomprehension and hits our off button. Today, the weather bureau tells us: 'The coastal area has been impacted by a weather event.' What's wrong with 'the storm hit the beach'? Businesses write on their websites: 'We apply uncommon ingenuity to deliver cross-enterprise results.' Perhaps they come up with clever ways to solve problems. So, why not say that?

Avoid acronyms, foreign words and corporate speak

Acronyms are also a barrier to understanding. When I interviewed an aeronautical expert, she referred to 'EASA', 'FAA' and 'CASA'. Unless you're an aviation expert, it's doubtful you'll know these terms. Spell out acronyms for the lay audience. Also, avoid a foreign word when there's a perfectly good English one. Although sometimes it can't be helped. Ballet, fashion and cooking are full of French words, classical music scores are written in Italian, and psychoanalysts love German terms such as 'Gestalt' and 'Schadenfreude'. But if you use foreign words unnecessarily, you'll risk alienating your audience.

Corporate speak is a language most professionals are well-versed in. Indeed, it's so pervasive that many in the corporate, political and legal worlds don't recognise it as jargon. They simply assume everyone understands phrases such as 'moving forward', 'taking it offline', 'onboarding', 'circling back', 'customer-centric' and 'process-driven'.

Author and former political speechwriter Don Watson calls this 'contemporary gibberish' and says: 'the language of business and work grow ever more depleted, barren and senseless.' He warns that corporate speak 'obscures the truth and erodes nuance and meaning'. It can confuse people and make it difficult for them to challenge and question the speaker.

If you've been speaking corporate lingo for a while and forgotten your mother tongue, check out the resources on the Plain English Foundation's website. You could also practise your messages with someone outside your industry and ask them to stop you each time you use an unfamiliar phrase.

Tell us a story

The way news and current affairs are presented has changed drastically in recent years. Audiences have always been drawn to stories, but with so much more content to enjoy from streaming services, social media, YouTube and podcasts, news programs need to compete for audiences by being as engaging as possible. While TV and radio news are always chasing quick sound bites and grabs, content producers of documentaries and long-form podcasts are seeking interviewees who can tell an engaging yarn. When it comes to interviewing talent, the top of a producer's wish list is someone who can relate a riveting anecdote, attention-grabbing example or illuminating analogy to illustrate the problem at hand.

Michelle Farrar is one such expert. She's a professor of paediatric neurology at the University of New South Wales and specialist child neurologist at Sydney Children's Hospital. I interviewed her about how groundbreaking gene therapy is reversing spinal muscular atrophy – a rare but crippling disorder in some babies.

Farrar used a clever analogy to explain how gene therapy works: 'You can't just give the gene to a person by injecting it, because it would be destroyed. So, it's like posting a letter, and the letter is the gene, and the envelope is an inactive virus. It delivers the gene into the nucleus … and it immediately starts working, and it keeps working. Then the envelope is put in the bin.'

She communicates this complex process in simple, visual terms without using technical, medical or scientific jargon.

Describe the benefits, not the features

Bruce Lambert from the Department of Health Communication in Chicago is also a master in simplifying complex concepts. He explains his own work around drug name confusion in scientific terms and then in language accessible to lay audiences. His tip is to focus on the benefits rather than the specific features.

Here's how he describes the scientific features: 'I can use a variety of different orthographic and phonological similarity measures to compute a numerical similarity score between those two representations and use that similarity score to predict the probability of confusion …'

Now here's how Lambert explains the benefits in plain English: 'About 4 million times per year, people walk into pharmacies in the United States and walk out with the wrong drug … because drug names are so similar, they're confusing. Out of these four million, a significant number get hurt because they take the wrong drug or because they fail to get the drug they need. My work helps fewer people get hurt.'

This tag line is gold: 'My work helps fewer people get hurt.' If you can summarise the benefits of your research/product/service in one line, you are conveying why your work matters.

A valuable exercise is to describe what you do at your next festive lunch or family gathering. If you can't explain to Aunt Rose what you do, clearly and briefly, how would you handle a media interview, speak confidently on a public panel or pitch for a grant from new investors? More importantly, it's not what you do but *why* you do it. For example:

- It's not that you study microbes in Antarctica; it's that you're searching for answers to climate change.
- It's not that you're simply researching ways to use AI in public transport; it's that you are designing more liveable cities.
- It's not only that you're breaking new ground in gene therapy; it's that you're improving the lives of children born with life-threatening conditions.
- It's not that you work in B2B systems analytics; it's that you help global companies communicate with their staff and customers more easily.

Tailor your message to your audience

It's vital to put yourself in the shoes of your audience or readers. Know your audience. Address their needs. Speak their language. If you're interviewed by a reporter from the *Australian Financial Review*, their readers are likely to be concerned about how rising interest rates will affect their investments, whereas readers of the *Daily Telegraph* might be more interested in tips for saving money on their weekly grocery bill.

If you're speaking to a reporter from *The West Australian*, they'll want to know how readers in Perth can access your product or service locally. Do your research. Make sure you know who their main football teams are, if it's relevant, and learn to pronounce local place names, especially if you're being interviewed on a regional radio station.

At one point, Channel Ten made a cost-saving decision to run their weekend news bulletins for Adelaide, Hobart and Perth out of their Sydney studio. There was an outcry from Adelaideans when the Sydney-based presenter pronounced the inner-city suburb of Thebarton as 'THE-Barton'. It might seem inconsequential, but the mispronunciation was literally a turn-off for Adelaide viewers. Channel Ten reconsidered its decision. Now, the Adelaide bulletin is produced in Melbourne. However, the reporters, camera crews and editorial staff are based in Adelaide.

Preparing your key messages

Now we're getting to the secret sauce of how to come up with quotable key messages. Ideally, you should have three bullet-proof key messages up your sleeve, ready to deliver no matter what you're asked.

These are the same structures we saw in chapter 3 for presentation skills. However, the way you deliver your message will be different depending on the medium and whether you're doing a live or pre-recorded interview.

Point, reason, example, so what?

Here's a real-life example from the former CEO of Cancer Council Australia, Sanchia Aranda, being interviewed on SKY News:

Point: The sun is particularly dangerous for Queenslanders.

Reason: The UV rating is above three on most days, which causes sun damage.

Example: Two out of three Australians will get skin cancer at some stage of their lives.

So what?: So, it's particularly important we pay attention to sun safety.

Aranda cuts through the vast volume of data around melanoma research and delivers one key statistic, one heart-stopping example and one simple and direct call to action. This is the gold standard for key message structures.

In this next example, Rebecca Jenkinson from the Australian Gambling Research Centre uses the same structure on breakfast television – but her last point isn't as effective. See if you can pinpoint why.

Point: All governments have a role to play here in restricting and reducing exposure to advertising.

> **Reason**: Our research has found that exposure to ads leads to riskier gambling behaviour and harm.
> **Example**: Especially, young people and people already at risk of harm.
> **So what?**: So, this is a real concern for us and the community is calling for action.

Jenkinson starts off well, but her call to action is vague. The community is calling for action. What action and by when? A better one would be: 'We're appealing to the government to ban gambling ads to protect young and vulnerable people.'

Point, reason, reason, reason, point

Candice Hughes is the in-house solicitor for YFS. I trained the YFS team and interviewed Candice about whether the Queensland government's new legislation to jail children as young as ten for serious crimes would reduce the rate of youth crime in that state. As you'll see, Candice shoots straight from the hip:

> **Point**: Tougher sentencing is a waste of money; it's a human rights abuse and won't reduce youth crime.
> **Reason**: These kids are stealing because they have nowhere to live and nothing to eat.
> **Reason**: It costs more than a million dollars a year to lock up kids, and 80 per cent will reoffend.
> **Reason**: Our mentoring program costs only $100 000 a year per child and has a 66 per cent reduction in repeat offences.

Point: If we want to reduce crimes, we need to address
the reasons kids are committing them.

Point, Counterpoint, Reason, Point

Only use this when the journalist has already raised an objection or opposing viewpoint. Professor Mimi Zou from UNSW Law & Justice is arguing for stricter AI regulations. To play devil's advocate, which journalists love to do, I asked if tighter regulation would restrain innovation. She used this effective structure to respond:

Point: Australia should take a more proactive approach
to regulating AI.
Counterpoint: While the US has a wait-and-see
approach because it fears stifling innovation, it is
out of step with the international consensus.
Reason: The EU has already taken the lead in the first
comprehensive AI legislation to minimise harm caused
by AI systems in high-risk areas.
Point: We need safeguards to protect our privacy
and prevent bias and prejudice, and the potential
significant harms that AI poses, before it's too late.

Point, Past, Present, Future, Point

The following example comes from my media training session with Professor Jason Grebely from the Kirby Institute at UNSW Sydney:

Point: Australia is on track to eliminate hepatitis C
thanks to a new finger-prick test that gives results in
less than an hour.
Past: In the past, hepatitis C has been a 'silent
disease' with poorly tolerated treatments.
Present: New treatments are 95 per cent successful in
8–12 weeks.
Future: This will position Australia as a global leader in
detecting, treating and preventing hepatitis C.
Point: This advancement is a game changer.

When crafting your key messages, use short bullet points. Don't waffle. These structures give you a logical flow to persuade your audience for or against your statement. Use statistics, examples, anecdotes and experience to support your main point.

Go into an interview armed with at least three of these prepared and rehearsed key messages. No matter what you're asked, use a key message up front to set the agenda. The other two can be used when the interview questions are veering off topic or you're caught like a deer in the headlights and don't know what to say.

The other way to get across your message is through a relevant story. Choosing this technique will depend on your subject, your audience and the medium platform. If you're speaking to commercial TV or radio news, use the above structures to craft a snappy, quotable statement. If you're speaking on a longer radio program, a documentary, a podcast or a panel, you can afford the time to connect with the audience through a story. Revisit the storytelling chapter of this book.

How journalists choose quotes or soundbites

In a pre-recorded interview, a journalist may grill you for 20 minutes and then choose a couple of grabs for a radio or TV news story. That doesn't mean the rest of what you've said is wasted; it might be paraphrased in the journalist's script. What makes a soundbite stand out? Often, the reporter will select an emotionally charged response or a message that cuts to the heart of the story. Here are some examples:

1. Superlatives
    »   'AI has the potential to be more transformative than electricity or fire.'
    »   'This is a once-in-a-generation opportunity for change.'
    »   'Australia has one of the highest rates of asthma in the world.'

2. Action
    »   'We are on the path to wiping out hepatitis C worldwide.'
    »   'We want wood heaters to hit the chopping block for cleaner air.'
    »   'We don't just solve customers' problems; we are constantly innovating and pre-empting problems that don't yet exist.'

3. Analogies, metaphors, stories
   » 'Sometimes being the boss is like running a cemetery:
     you've got a lot of people under you, but nobody's
     listening.'
   » 'The ASX 200 rebounded with all the hallmarks of
     a dead cat bounce.'
   » 'Fossil fuels are like spending your savings –
     once you use them up, they're gone.'

Most journalists will know when they hear the right quote. It's as if a little bell goes off in their heads and they think, *Ah – that's it!*

I explained it to my journalism students like this: imagine you bump into an old friend you haven't seen for ages, and you catch up on each other's news during a 20-minute chat. When you go home, you might relay the highlights of that conversation to someone else. You'll probably select different snippets, depending on whether you speak to your mother, partner, kids or another friend. You'll know instinctively what your audience will be interested in.

ABC journalist Anne Connolly reported in a *Four Corners* program how thousands of vulnerable Australians under the guardianship of the Public Trustee can lose control over their money and assets or rights to appeal.

Connolly relied on three main subject matter experts to explain much of the story through interview sound bites. She chose the strongest quote for the 'promo' to encourage viewers to tune in to the program. 'This can happen to you. All you have to do is have a fall, or have a temporary brain injury, or be admitted to hospital and you could find yourself under

Public Guardian orders with your life decisions taken away from you.'

Connolly explained why she chose that grab. 'This makes the story relatable to every single person watching, so that people think, I should watch this program, because what if this happens to me or a loved one?'

In interviews, there's certainly room for subject matter experts to express their thoughts and tell a relevant story that draws on their experience. Retired fire chief Greg Mullins grabbed Australians' attention when he called the 2019–20 Black Summer bushfires 'unprecedented'. Mullins is the country's longest-serving fire commissioner and there's no arguing with his credentials. Since then, Mullins has become a climate activist. He has turbo-charged his message by making it personal. 'It's gonna be a very, very dangerous place to live – not Australia, planet Earth,' Mullins said. 'I'm deeply worried about my grandsons and what they're inheriting from us.'

When respected officials use their credentials to underpin a weighty point, it can be a powerful wake-up call. Honest accounts like these can shake up and improve emergency procedures and policies.

Interview dos and don'ts

Do pass on questions that are outside your area of expertise. You can't have the answers to everything all the time. Stick to your lane and area of knowledge. Tell the interviewer to ask the minister that question, or your colleague in finance, or someone who has that personal experience, then link to a key message.

Do ask the interviewer to clarify their question. This can buy you time to think. Journalists sometimes ask waffly questions, and this is the perfect opportunity to say, 'Would you mind repeating the question, please?' If a reporter asks a double-barrelled question, simply respond to the question you'd prefer to answer. The journalist can follow up on the other one if they want to.

Do politely correct the interviewer if they have their facts wrong. Don't allow myths or inaccuracies to persist. Another media outlet may have incorrectly quoted or reported on this issue. Now it's your opportunity to set the record straight. Tell them you're not sure where they found those statistics, because your research/experience shows otherwise, then hit them with the facts.

Do use plain English and clear, relevant examples. Jargon and acronyms are a turn-off and may mean your interview is cut from the podcast or TV/radio report.

Do ask the journalist if they need more information and follow up. This is an opportunity to give them a background briefing (an executive summary, not a 300-page report) to ensure they have accurate, relevant and up-to-date data from a reliable source.

Don't fudge statistics or lie. You'd be surprised how some people prefer to make up the answer rather than simply say they don't know. If you lie, it will come back to bite you. There's no shame in saying, 'I don't have those statistics right now. I can get back to you with those, but what I do know is …' And then give them some figures you are certain about.

Don't take the bait or get wound up – it's not personal. You may remember the infamous TV interview with the former

CEO of Woolworths, Brad Banducci. When the reporter asked him if Woolworths and Coles were a duopoly that engaged in price fixing, the CEO stood up and walked out. It was a PR disaster. Instead, he should have calmly explained the factors that had contributed to higher prices.

Communication strategist Stephen Watson agrees. 'If you're sitting in a TV studio, you might feel like you're being subjected to an overly aggressive line of questioning; the reality is for the viewing audience, that it won't seem that way at all. You mustn't overreact.'

Don't feel the need to fill the silence. Occasionally, interviewers will use silence to rattle you or to prompt you to say more than you should. Say your piece and then stop. Don't keep talking. That's the job of the interviewer, not you.

Don't say anything off the record or be seduced into speculating on hypothetical situations. Journalists love to speculate. What if we have another pandemic? What if cyberhackers sell our bank details on the dark web? What if the next bushfire is worse than the last? Nobody has a crystal ball. It's a mug's game to dabble in fortune-telling. Simply stick to the facts at hand and talk about what's working and what you and your team are doing to make the situation better.

Don't ask to see a copy before it's published. Journalists fear if they have to wait for you to check their copy, they'll miss their deadline. Instead, offer to check their facts. If the story is highly technical, this could help them out.

Don't give guarantees or say, 'No comment.' If you've agreed to an interview, you must come up with something intelligent to say. This is why it's vital to practise your key messages and link back to them when the questions become awkward.

Don't let your eyes wander. If you're presenting or speaking to a journalist online, look straight at the camera on the computer. If you're speaking to a reporter in person, look at them, *not* at the camera. However, if you are doing a 'live cross', the studio producer will ask you to look down the barrel of the camera. And don't look down at your notes or phone, because then you lose eye contact and connection with your audience.

Finally, don't let reporters put words in your mouth. Most journalists have the gift of the gab. They use catchy phrases that are easy to repeat. But if you use their phrase, the producer will edit out the question for a short TV or radio soundbite and it will sound as if the quote was solely your idea. Stick to your own script.

CHAPTER 6

Control techniques and crisis media

We've seen how it works when an interview is going well, but what about when the journalist leads you off track with irrelevant questions, or strays into controversial no-go areas? My advice is to stay calm and pivot. You do this by partially answering the question, making that 20 per cent of your response, and then using a bridging phrase to link back to your key message.

When you panic and speak on a topic you're not 100 per cent sure about, that's when you can make mistakes. You don't have to have an answer for everyone, on all things, all the time. Preparing for an interview requires strategic thinking, practice and discipline.

Dr Meraiah Foley and her team at the University of Sydney Business School have secured widespread media coverage for their research on sexual harassment in the retail industry. I asked Meraiah what their winning formula was for scoring accurate, on-point reporting.

'We laid out the research very clearly and had an executive summary in plain English that any educated layperson could understand. Avoiding academic jargon is really important, and then also translating that into good talking points for the media release also helps,' Foley said. 'We do a lot of preparation before we talk to the media. It takes work to prepare and think through clearly what the key points are and what I want to convey in this interview, ensuring I stay on point, regardless of what question is served up to me. It takes practice to pivot from a question that maybe isn't exactly the question you want to answer to the point you want to make.'

Control techniques

So, how exactly do you pivot back into the driver's seat of the interview? By using bridging phrases or linking lines. Here are some examples you can use:

- 'That's a fair question, but what's important to remember here is …'
- 'That's not my area; you'd have to ask the minister that or someone in cybersecurity, but what I can tell you about the work we're doing here is …'
- 'That's a common misconception; however, our 20 years in the business shows us … or our customers tell us that …'
- 'I'm not sure where those statistics come from, but what we know from research or experience is …'
- 'That's an interesting point; however, we're focused on …'
- 'I'm unable to comment on any allegations under investigation. We are, however, committed to …'
- 'I don't have those statistics right now. I'm happy to get back to you with those. But what we do know is this …'

Politicians are notorious for evading questions. It can be maddening – for audiences and journalists alike. Journalist Anne Connolly has seen this tactic many times. 'Some politicians are extremely experienced in not answering the question. They give long-winded answers. They use formal language. They go off on different tangents. And they make it almost impossible for you to get a grab. They know exactly what they're doing.'

Both sides of politics employ this device. When women marched in towns and cities around the country to protest against gender-based violence, Prime Minister Anthony Albanese turned up to one of the rallies and gave an impromptu speech. But there was some dispute as to whether or not he'd been invited to speak. The organisers took to social media to vent their frustration. The next morning on TV news, he was asked to set the record straight. The Prime Minister ignored the question and went straight to his key message: 'I think the important issue here is that yesterday and the day before and the day before that, Australians rallied in their tens of thousands, saying enough is enough.'

If you're the prime minister, you can often get away with not answering the question unless it's during a crisis, as former prime minister Scott Morrison learned during the 2019–20 bushfires. People who'd lost their homes demanded the government act on climate change. Morrison replied: 'There is a time and a place to debate controversial issues and important issues, right now it's important to focus on the needs of Australians who need our help.'

So, how can you, as a spokesperson, learn from politicians' interview strategies without selling your soul? A better way is to briefly acknowledge the question and then bridge back to your message. Alternatively, you can hit pause on a problematic story. You might need to tell a journalist you're not comfortable being quoted on a specific topic because it's not your area of expertise, but instead you can provide some background, so they'll better understand a complex issue.

Meraiah Foley used this method to 'kill' a potentially inflammatory and inaccurate story. A reporter rang asking her for a comment about a large organisation that had sent a cautionary email to its workers, warning of the potential risks of having an OnlyFans account. The email did not condemn or forbid this activity but rather pointed out the conflict of interest it could pose, especially if staff were to encounter their fans in the course of their work. Foley sensed the journalist was on the hunt for a juicy clickbait story. 'I did not want to be quoted as a gender equality scholar saying it's totally okay for employers to slut-shame their employees. But I did want to encourage this journalist to understand the issue was much more complicated,' Foley said.

Foley explained to the reporter that case law is still evolving as to what employers can and can't demand of their employees' social media use in their private lives. Unless you sign a contract, an employer can't dictate what you say or do as a private citizen on social media, but they can draw some reasonable and defensible boundaries around how their staff represent their organisation, especially while wearing a uniform.

In the end, the journalist didn't write the story. A case of no news is good news. So, don't be afraid to draw boundaries around the areas you're prepared to be quoted on. This strategy works best in the pre-interview stage, when you're talking on the phone to a journalist, during the so-called 'fishing expedition', when the reporter is assessing whether the story is worth pursuing and whether you're good talent. It might be harder to persuade the journalist to hit the pause button if you're already being recorded for TV or radio. You can, however, ask for the camera or microphone to be switched off while you explain your concerns. If you're in the middle of a live broadcast interview, it's obviously too late. You'll need to use your bridging lines to get back on track. At the same time, don't come across as defensive; you can still be firm while being friendly and informative.

How to handle a media crisis

Think about some of the big names in business and industry. Why do you remember them? Chances are, it's for the wrong reasons. Have their names been splashed across media headlines because they were involved in a scandal involving sex, money, drugs or bullying? It's an unedifying fact about humans that we love salacious gossip. Did you know the name of the former CEO of Woolworths before he walked out of an ABC interview about price fixing? Did you know who the new CEO of Qantas was before she faced questions about a cyberattack? What do you remember about a certain celebrity chef after the courts ordered him to pay back thousands in unpaid wages? As American businessman and philanthropist Warren Buffett once said: 'It takes 20 years to build a reputation and five minutes to ruin it.'

If you were one of the 10 million Australians caught up in the Optus service outage, how did you feel about the way the CEO handled it? Or if your personal details were stolen in the Medibank data breach, how reassured did you feel that everything was being done to restore order? If you were a parent with a pre-schooler in childcare, did you feel panicked by the arrest of a childcare worker on paedophile charges? And if you were one of the millions of passengers caught in the mayhem at Heathrow airport after its electricity substation caught on fire, how did you feel about the airport's CEO going to bed while chaos and confusion reigned?

Despite our best intentions, things can and will go wrong in businesses, institutions and organisations. Tech failures, faulty products, creative accounting, workplace accidents, sexual harassment complaints and staff posting inappropriate videos on social media – it's a minefield. It's not whether something will happen to your organisation to tarnish your reputation. It's how you deal with it that will make or break your reputation. Gone are the days when heads of large companies could duck under their desks and wait until the storm passed. If you don't deal with a crisis head-on, it can blow up in the media and become an even greater headache. And the buck always stops with the CEO or top brass. But the good news is that if you have a plan, keep your cool, are transparent and sincere in your messaging, and everyone in your organisation sings from the same songbook, you can win back public trust sooner rather than later.

If a crisis occurs, especially a workplace accident or fatality, you should issue a holding statement to the media and your staff within the first 30 to 45 minutes. A holding statement

– either written or spoken – verifies the known facts and literally holds off the barrage of media enquiries until you have more information. If officials such as the police, firefighters, ASIO or ASIC are called in to investigate, then you can't speculate or say anything to the media or your staff that's not yet proven, because you could inadvertently influence a future jury if the matter ends up in court.

In this case, the best policy is to say to media enquiries: 'I can't comment on any of those details while police are examining the evidence and conducting interviews; however, I can say we are doing X to secure the scene/protect the public/ keep customers informed/cooperate with authorities.'

If you have a gaggle of journalists, photographers and camera crews camped on your doorstep, address them calmly with your prepared holding statement. Here are some guidelines:

- Introduce yourself and set the agenda.
- Pause, breathe, think.
- Express concern and compassion for affected families and colleagues.
- Confirm basic authorised details of the incident, with the verified facts.
- Explain what happened.
- Explain when and where it occurred.
- Explain who was affected. Don't release names of the injured or deceased until the police have contacted all family members and given clearance to name them publicly.
- Describe the action you have taken or are about to take.
- Mention policies, safety and investigation.

- Don't speculate or comment on any rumours.
- Be authoritative while remaining compassionate and authentic.
- Commit to updating journalists within the hour and then regularly as the situation unfolds and more details come to hand.
- Say you need to get back to the scene and exit quickly without taking further questions.

Leave the 'why' and 'how' the accident occurred for later, perhaps days or weeks later, for the inevitable news analysis and 'what have we learned' opinion pieces. You should also issue a written holding statement on your website and platforms such as LinkedIn and Facebook. Issue a media release via a service such as Medianet, Scoop, Newswire or Business Wire. For example:

> At 6 am this morning, our tech team at XYZ company alerted us to a cyber breach on our website. We believe some of our customers' personal details may have been compromised. We don't yet know whether that includes customer credit card details.
>
> We have a cyber team working around the clock to secure the site. For those customers who are concerned, we invite them to call this hotline or to stay up to date via our social media feed and website.

The holding statement gives the media the bare facts, so they can file a story. If you don't say anything, journalists will use guerrilla tactics to get information. They'll camp outside your office, university, council chambers and 'doorstop' staff as they enter and leave the building. Doorstopping is exactly as it sounds. A reporter with a microphone and maybe a camera operator arrives unannounced to interrogate you or your staff as you enter or leave the building. I've doorstopped a couple of prime ministers, many politicians and a host of lawyers and citizens leaving courtrooms. It's rarely a satisfactory experience for either party. It's best to be on the front foot and organise a media conference after the holding statement, and when you have more useful information to divulge. If you're doorstopped and run, the public will assume the worst.

Dodging questions looks dodgy

Do you remember the 2017 Royal Commission into Misconduct in the Banking, Superannuation and Financial Services Industry? The bankers spent all day listening to and answering questions during the inquiry, but once they stepped outside the building, they bowed their heads and ran for cover to avoid the waiting journalists with their cameras and microphones. Of course, facing the media can be daunting. But when the bosses of two of the biggest banks pretended they couldn't see the media pack or hear their questions (e.g. Why did you pay massive bonuses to executives who were acting illegally? Why did you charge fees to deceased customers' accounts?), it reinforced the public perception that bankers were arrogant, greedy and didn't give two hoots about their customers. It was a PR disaster. Along with listening to their lawyers, they should have listened to their PR and media advisers.

Finally, the former head of Westpac, Brian Hartcher, stepped out and said a few words to the media. 'It's been good to speak to the commission today. It's been a very rigorous and valuable process. We are committed that where we haven't got things right for customers, we'll put it right. Thank you for your interest.' He then walked away with some dignity, without looking back. He didn't say much of substance, just mouthed a few platitudes, but at least he stopped and spoke.

How to communicate during a media crisis

Imagine you are the PR and marketing officer for a local council. It's your job to communicate with residents about what's happening in the hood. It's always a pleasure to tell a good news story to ratepayers, either via a media release or social media post: 'New dog park has tails wagging', 'Giant tube slide in playground is a hit with kids', 'Disability groups praise renovated library for easy access'.

But what happens when things go wrong? A dog viciously attacks a senior citizen. A swing collapses and injures a child. A librarian refuses access to a guide dog.

Unfortunately, residents are more likely to criticise rather than praise, and if their complaint isn't resolved, they may take to social media to vent. When tempers run high, facts are usually the first casualty.

Senior Brisbane City councillor David McLachlan says he uses the council's Facebook and X accounts as a barometer for what's bothering residents. 'It's like the canary in the coal mine,' McLachlan says. If a disgruntled resident is bellyaching on the council's Facebook page, McLachlan recommends the following statement to take the heat out of the argument before the post goes viral:

Dear Sandy (use their first name),

Thank you for bringing this issue to our attention. Unfortunately, regulations prevent me from using this platform to discuss council matters. I'd be happy to correspond with you via official council channels during office hours.

I look forward to hearing from you.

This approach usually de-escalates the matter temporarily; however, if the issue is not dealt with promptly, it may attract negative media attention. Nobody wants a TV news crew doorstopping them outside the council chambers. The media can make or break an organisation's reputation overnight, so it pays to be prepared.

If you want to stay in the driver's seat, you'll need to prepare two or three key messages and make sure they're watertight. If an accident, data breach or other misadventure occurs, you have a responsibility to your constituents, stakeholders and staff to communicate the facts clearly and promptly. Get the jump on the media and keyboard warriors by issuing a holding statement within the hour. For example: 'At 1.35 this afternoon, we received a call from a resident claiming two preschool children were injured riding the new giant tube slide at the Hamilton Street Playground. The children were taken by ambulance to Southwest Hospital and are in a stable condition.' (Don't release names or details of the injuries at this point until police have alerted all family members.)

After you deliver your holding statement, don't take any questions. Thank the media for their interest and commit to updating them within the hour or later that day when you have more details from police, the hospital and/or the engineers.

The danger of *not* issuing an official statement is that journalists will go fishing for someone else to interview – the family, eyewitnesses, neighbours, hospital staff or a member of the opposition who might insinuate the council has cut corners in constructing the giant tube slide. When you have more information, use this proven structure for either a face-to-face interview or a written media statement:

- **Care**. Convey your heartfelt condolences to the children, their family and anyone else who witnessed this distressing event. Be authentic. Avoid saying 'our thoughts and prayers are with the family'. It's a cliché that every politician uses. Imagine what you would want to hear if you were in the shoes of the bereaved or affected family.
- **Action**. Say what you're doing to fix the problem. For example, 'We have closed the playground, and our engineers and maintenance crews are conducting a full investigation into what went wrong with the new equipment.'
- **Message**. What is it you want your audience to know? For example, 'The safety of all our residents

is paramount, and we will ensure the equipment is repaired to the highest standards and checked and re-checked before we consider re-opening the playground.'
- **Perspective**. Is there anything that went relatively well in this scenario? For example, 'We thank the quick-thinking resident who called an ambulance and alerted our maintenance crew, which responded immediately to secure the area.'
- **Stick to it**. Don't speculate as to what caused the accident or what might happen in the future.

Think about the types of questions you'll be asked and prepare for them. Journalists' questions usually start with what, where, when, why, who or how? Workshop all the possible questions with a colleague and practise your responses. Remember, you don't have to answer *all* of them, especially if they involve laying blame. Use your linking lines to get back on track to your key messages. Here's a sample of the types of questions you may face:

- What is the extent of the children's injuries?
- How did the accident occur?
- Should there be a height restriction for children using the tube slide?
- Are you expecting their parents to sue the council?
- Will you remove the giant tube slide permanently?
- Is this what happens when you outsource construction projects?
- Other councils have banned giant tube slides, saying they are too dangerous; will you follow suit?

- Does the council take full responsibility for this accident?

Rather than being seduced into speculation, simply say: 'We won't know how or why this happened until we've conducted a full investigation.' Don't give any guarantees. There are no guarantees in life except death and taxes.

Here's an example of how one of my clients, a company whose share price plummeted during COVID, used this structure to convey its message to its staff, shareholders and clients through a financial news platform:

- **Care**: 'Yes, we can understand investors' and shareholders' frustration with this latest downturn.
  Action. Our company has made significant and positive changes to our leadership roles, business models and client demonstrations, all of which we're confident will boost our performance and share price.
  Message. We've been growing steadily for 30 years, and our teams are both experienced and innovative. More than 90 per cent of our customers choose to stay with us when they see the value we add to their business.
  Perspective. IT companies worldwide are struggling to attract and retain skilled staff. There have been many challenges for businesses since the pandemic. We're not alone in that.
- **Stick to it**. Don't get tricked into commenting on hypotheticals or speculating on the future. For example, 'We don't know what the future holds, but we are confident in our people and our processes.'

Reputation management

It's also vital to keep employees and customers up to date with everything you know *before* you speak to journalists. Fewer things peeve staff and clients more than finding out in the media, rather than from their bosses, about fraud allegations or impending redundancies. They feel betrayed, taken for granted and excluded. Nothing spreads faster than outrage, hurt and anger. If you're transparent about what's happening and make your staff and shareholders feel included, they'll be your best allies and ambassadors. Shut them out and they'll become a hit squad. Once upon a time, journalists wanting to dig up dirt would go through an accused staff member's rubbish bin. Now, it's as simple as scanning social media posts and comments by disgruntled staff, customers and clients. The only mob angrier than confused staff are dissatisfied customers.

Robyn Sefiani is a senior communications professional and reputation and crisis manager. Her role is to help corporate clients and high-profile individuals build, enhance and protect their brands and reputations. That's the easy part of the job. The difficult part is defending brands and reputations through difficult times, and like it or not, almost every organisation will face a crisis or issue at some stage. 'This is really where reputations are tested when things go wrong, and particularly where organisations have not anticipated that something might go wrong and they've not prepared for it,' Sefiani says. The good news is that you can prepare for a media crisis.

'Every crisis manager talks about the three Rs – readiness, response and repair, or rebuild the reputation if it's been damaged through the crisis. And there's no doubt in my mind that the real focus has to be on readiness,' Sefiani says. 'I've been a crisis manager and reputation manager for over three decades, and in every single situation where we've worked with a client through a crisis, if the client is prepared, they will more successfully navigate the crisis and come out the other end with their reputation pretty much intact.'

Sefiani's team works with their clients to ensure they're prepared. The first step is to identify all potential risks to their organisation. 'Think about the things that keep you awake at night that you hope will never happen and that would have the biggest negative impact on your company's brand or reputation,' Sefiani says.

The list of possible disasters is long. A company could be the victim of a ransomware attack, or a manufacturer might lose all its stock in a massive warehouse fire. An aged care facility or a cruise company could experience a mass outbreak of gastroenteritis or COVID. Sefiani knows the worst-case scenarios for everyone:

> If it's a professional services firm, it's going to be something like allegations of sexual harassment, racism or bullying. If it's a publicly listed company, it might be a hostile takeover attempt or a major walk-out of your senior executive team to a competitor. For an aviation company, it would be an aircraft crash. Every industry is going to have particular crisis scenarios that would cause either death, huge business interruption, upheaval and loss of reputation.

After identifying potential risks, you need to understand which stakeholders will be impacted. Are they customers, clients, policymakers, employees or potential employees? Who is going to matter most, and who do you need to talk to first in a crisis?

The next step, according to Sefiani, is to roll out the communications plan and establish who will be on the crisis management team. 'Every organisation needs at least one nominated spokesperson who's fully media trained – not six months ago, but right up to the minute. Ideally, there's also a backup person in case the nominated spokesperson is on leave, unwell or overseas.'

The spokesperson will respond when the bad news lands, whether that's via a phone call or email from a journalist who's been contacted by a whistleblower with allegations of bullying, or a phone call from the police saying someone has died at one of your work sites. Someone in the C-suite will usually be the spokesperson. If it's a really big crisis, it will be the CEO. If it's a cyber breach, it might be the CTO, and if a nursing home is flooded and the residents are evacuated, the COO will be across all the logistics.

It's a good idea for members of the crisis communications team to set up a group chat on WhatsApp, Slack, Telegram or Signal to easily update each other and make fast decisions across multiple time zones. 'When a crisis occurs, you don't have very much time to respond,' Sefiani tells her clients. 'You've got to get a statement out within half an hour, because if you don't, others will fill the vacuum.'

The Optus cyber hack in 2022, its network outage a year later and the fatal triple-0 call failures are textbook case studies of how *not* to handle a PR disaster. The Optus data breach in September 2022 affected about 10 000 current and former customers. With a lack of real leadership or clear communication from the top, customers became concerned, then alarmed and finally angry. It led to a mass exodus of customers and a damaged company reputation.

Sefiani describes this as a classic case of management not taking the lead. 'It was one weekday morning. People were beside themselves, wanting to know what was happening. But Optus was silent. So, the then Federal Minister for Communications, Michelle Rowland, went on breakfast TV and said, "I'm calling on Optus to say something, to tell people what's going on with their network."'

Even if you aren't 100 per cent sure of all the details, it's vital to acknowledge that something has occurred, and you're doing everything in your power to get to the bottom of it and will update customers and stakeholders as soon as you have more information. People need to know a steady pair of hands is steering the ship and that the captain hasn't jumped overboard and left a rudderless vessel heading for the rocks, with the blindfolded crew still on board.

If there's been a death, then the CEO must front up to the media and reach out to the bereaved. The 2016 Dreamworld tragedy on the Gold Coast, in which four people died on the Thunder River Rapids ride, was the worst theme park accident in Australia's history since the 1979 Luna Park fire. The owner of Dreamworld is Ardent Leisure, and at the time, Deborah Thomas was at its helm. She was widely criticised for not contacting the families after the accident. It's a faux pas she's since apologised for, and she's tried to make amends.

But for the grieving families, a perceived snub such as that, can be hard to forgive and forget.

During a crisis, it's also prudent to be aware of what others are saying about you. It's a case of keeping your friends close and your enemies closer. Sefiani recommends a central team in your organisation to monitor and gather feedback from social media, talkback radio and other customer channels. That allows you to be strategic about what messages you direct to key stakeholders, rather than broadcasting every detail to the world. For small organisations without a communications team, they can hire an agency to temporarily monitor all channels and send them hourly update reports.

Monitoring social media during a crisis is not for the faint-hearted. However, it has its uses. Sefiani offers this advice: 'With social media monitoring, you've got to be really careful. It's what we call community management. If people on your Facebook or Instagram are making direct, nasty comments about you, it's better not to engage directly, but you can say, "We're concerned to hear this. Please contact us at this email, because it's important to us and we'd like to respond to you directly." In that way, you take it offline.'

When the immediate crisis wanes, it's time to rebuild trust in your brand. 'A crisis is often born out of a poor culture. And that can be anywhere. It can be a school, a university, a corporation, or a not-for-profit,' Sefiani says. 'As a reputation manager, I will never be a messenger for someone who is deceitful or doing a cover-up. I have to be certain about the facts. It's not just about what you're going to say, it's more important to know what you are going to do now that this has happened.'

These days, the emergence of AI and deepfakes has added another layer of complexity, spurring a new type of online reputation management. The results of the Romanian election in November 2024 were turfed out when it was revealed Russia had employed TikTok ads, deepfakes and AI bots to promote a pro-Putin candidate. While fake accounts were consistently used throughout the campaign, one IT analyst revealed almost 30 000 fake TikTok and Instagram accounts were activated in the last 24 hours alone, generating 2.5 million comments in favour of the pro-Russian candidate. The accounts were traced to so-called 'bot farms' in Turkey using Russian domains.

Knowing what's true and what's not is becoming a challenge for companies, governments and also crisis communicators. But failing to plan is planning to fail. No matter what type of crisis may befall you, be prepared. Know who will be your spokesperson and how you will respond. Media training is one of the smartest insurance policies you can invest in.

CHAPTER 7

The power of inclusion

According to the recent Women in Media Gender Scorecard, only 30 per cent of expert sources quoted in news stories are women. That figure was less than half when it came to quoting experts in sport, motoring and defence. Men even dominated as media sources in industries where most of the employees were women, such as retail, health and education.

Women in Media is a registered charity representing women working in all types of Australian media, including journalism, PR, production and digital marketing. For several years, they've commissioned research to analyse almost 20 000 TV, radio and press news reports over a two-week period to understand how women are portrayed, featured and included as experts in their field.

Petra Buchanan, strategic adviser to Women in Media, says the scorecard is a wake-up call. 'We want more women to be seen and heard in the media and called on for their expert opinions, comments and reactions to better represent the society we live in,' she says.

But it's not just media interviews where women are less visible or audible. According to the founder of the Australian Women Speakers directory Jules Brooke, when corporate associations hire a speaker or MC for their business lunch or dinner event, they choose men over women 70 per cent of the time. That's prompted a few savvy businesswomen like Jules to set up female-only speaker directories and bureaus.

So, if women make up 51 per cent of the population, why aren't their voices making up at least half of the choir? An experienced Sydney-based lawyer told me she'd been invited to speak on radio about a significant case she'd been working on for months. She was the most qualified person to comment on its wider implications. However, she lacked the confidence to speak on live radio, so she declined the invitation. Instead, her junior male colleague jumped at the chance. The next morning, when she tuned in to the interview, she was shocked to hear him covering up sizeable gaps in his knowledge with vague generic statements and outright inaccuracies. But he sounded self-assured and unflappable. Back in the chambers, the young man was heralded as a hero. The senior female lawyer learned a valuable lesson that day and vowed never to pass up another opportunity to speak about her work again.

But it's unlikely the gender visibility gap is due merely to a lack of confidence. While Gen Z girls are being encouraged more than ever before to speak up at home, university and work, they are rarely sought out for their opinion or comments by traditional media. Then again, neither are young men.

A 2019 research report found only 11 per cent of news stories included the views or experiences of young people. Usually, their inclusion was through adult mediators such as parents, police or experts. And just 1% per cent of news stories directly quoted a young person. The study funded by the Museum of Australian Democracy, Google Australia and Western Sydney University analysed almost 300 news stories across eight national, state and regional newspapers, plus four national and state television news bulletins, during a week. No wonder young people feel disconnected from mainstream media.

I spoke to 26-year-old Toowoomba-based News Corp journalist, Jessica Klein, about how she felt writing for a medium her friends don't read or that doesn't include their opinions. 'I think one of the main reasons young people don't engage with traditional media is it doesn't really resonate with them. In traditional media, when we're reporting on young people, we're reporting about them, not with them. It's always adults talking. It's never their point of view.' Jessica says. 'Young people also think there is some sort of agenda with traditional media. Another thing is their short attention spans. If it's not a 10–15-second video, they're probably just going to keep scrolling.'

In 2024, Klein won the Caroline Jones Women in Media Young Journalist's Award. Besides reporting on local news and court stories in the Southern Downs and Granite Belt area of southwest Queensland, she's written extensively on regional social justice issues, including homelessness and domestic violence. She's interviewed inmates at the women's jail near Gatton and reported on mistreatment in an aged care centre. It's a shame so few of Jessica's friends read her award-winning stories in the *Warwick Daily News* and *Toowoomba Chronicle*.

In a bid to capture a younger audience, News Corp has posted some content on social media, a point Jessica impresses on her peers. 'I try to encourage them to at least participate in some sort of media. You can still absorb news in a 30-second TikTok video or Instagram reel. But it's rare that I see anyone under the age of 30 engaging with any of our content.'

Jessica is also encouraging the *Warwick Daily News* to create more posts that aren't behind a paywall to attract younger eyeballs. 'It's definitely something all newsrooms could improve on, because today's young people are going to be our next generation of leaders. So, we want them to be as best-informed as they can be. We need to engage them now, so when they're older, they'll still want to participate.'

Twenty-six-year-old SBS digital video producer Pranjali Sehgal agrees. 'Gen Z and millennials are not watching TV. They're going to digital sources because their phone is in their hand all the time. It's where they live and breathe, it's what's natural to them,' she says.

According to a 2023 research paper by the University of Canberra's News and Media Research Centre, news avoidance is high in Australia compared with other similar countries, but it's particularly high among young females, with 72 per cent of Gen Z women avoiding news, compared to 67 per cent of men.

One news platform that's plugging the gap is *Missing Perspectives*, which reaches more than a million young women every month through their podcasts, newsletters, videos and social channels. Two of their content creators even scored invitations to the federal budget lock-up in Canberra in 2025.

Two other prominent podcasts with a similar mission are *It's a Lot,* presented by former reality TV show star Abbie Chatfield, and *Big Small Talk*, hosted by Hannah Ferguson and Sarah Jane Adams. The latter's tag line is: 'Because, if you haven't realised, loving pop culture doesn't mean you don't understand politics.'

Twenty-four-year-old Hannah Ferguson told *HerCanberra Magazine*: 'I see myself as a commentator, not a journalist, not a lawyer, and not someone who's an expert in women's rights issues – I'm someone who sees a complex issue and knows how to communicate it simply with people. That's my passion.'

The podcasts and their associated YouTube and social accounts have more than a million followers, capturing the younger demographic in a way that mainstream Australian media can only dream of. This hasn't escaped politicians' attention either. In the 2025 election campaign, Prime Minister Anthony Albanese was interviewed on both podcasts. Abbie Chatfield spoke to him for 90 minutes on a variety of topics, from climate change to his engagement to Jodie Haydon. She also interviewed former Greens leader Adam Bandt.

During the same period, SBS hosted an online debate between six popular political social media influencers on a range of issues from housing affordability to climate action. No matter what your views, their level of passion and energy was kilowatts above the prime minister's and the opposition leader's televised debates.

In researching this book, I spoke to several young journalists and youth-focused news content creators. They display curiosity, drive and chutzpah and seem prepared to ask the awkward questions many older journalists ignore.

So, while there are now more alternative platforms to amplify the voices of women and young people, there are still others who we rarely hear from. Research in 2022 by Media Diversity Australia revealed that 80 per cent of the television news and current affairs presenters on the free-to-air networks were Anglo-Celtic. The *Who Gets to Tell Australian Stories?* report found only 6 per cent of on-air talent are from a non-European background, even though they comprise 25 per cent of the population.

SBS digital video producer Pranjali Sehgal says traditional media often stereotypes people from ethnic backgrounds rather than seeking them out for their expert opinions or giving them a voice on issues that affect all Australians.

'Young people and multicultural communities are often pigeonholed into certain narratives when they're so much more than that. They're professors, they're experts, they're people with lived experiences who can speak about what they've been through. Their perspective is very much missing from mainstream media,' she says.

Sehgal says when journalists don't seek out these communities for comments, it only compounds old tropes. 'It not only lowers the representation of young people and multicultural communities advocating for themselves in the media, but it also doubles down on the perception that these communities aren't engaged. They're not given the opportunities and platforms other people take for granted,' she says.

When she's not working at SBS, Sehgal is the head of media for Raise Our Voice, an organisation aimed at involving young people in politics and democracy through education, campaigns and communities. Sehgal is optimistic that perspectives are shifting in the media and society in general.

She says if you feel your expertise is being overlooked because you're young or have an ethnic background or disability, she recommends building your profile through

LinkedIn or other social media, blogging or podcast channels. Sehgal also suggests reaching out to the media to let them know you're available to speak as an authority on a specific topic if the opportunity arises.

Making your voice heard

If you've read this far, hopefully you have a much better understanding of how to play the media game to win. You know how to identify what makes a story or issue newsworthy.

You recognise what makes a stand-out presenter and media spokesperson and how to structure succinct, logical key messages. You've seen the techniques for staying on track by bridging back with linking lines, and you've grasped the value of telling a relevant, personal story to engage your audience. And you'll know how to effectively use your facial expressions, gestures, eye contact and voice.

Now, you're raring to go. You're ready to step up to the microphone. You have the expertise, the passion and the skills. The only thing missing is the opportunity. So far, no one has invited you to speak. In an earlier era, you may have stood on a soapbox in Speakers' Corner in Hyde Park to deliver a stirring sermon, to persuade and attract followers to your cause. Now you can do all that from the comfort of your own computer or phone. But the range of choices can be bewildering.

If you're not keen to start your own podcast or YouTube channel or lure subscribers to your blog on Substack, there are plenty of other options. Start by researching where your story or idea would best fit and suit the audience. You could write an op-ed piece for a newspaper, offer your expert opinion to a trade magazine, or pitch your angle to a radio interview or podcast.

When I was promoting my first book, I did 13 radio interviews back-to-back in two days. One of the best interviews was with a volunteer community radio presenter. She'd read my book cover to cover and asked more detailed questions than some of the professional journalists. A community radio or podcast interview can be a great way to practise your key messages and hone your interview skills before you approach mainstream media. You'll need to pitch a newsworthy angle. Send a media release with some attention-grabbing statistics, talking points and key messages that the radio producers and editors can grasp quickly.

When Sara Howard, founder of copywriting agency Writers Australia, launched her first business book, *Beyond Solo,* she soon realised social media posts weren't enough to boost book sales. She hired a publicist for two months to pitch different angles to targeted audiences via media releases and follow-up phone calls. One angle that picked up traction was debunking the myth that you have to retire to enjoy a sea or tree change. The online magazine *Inside Small Business* loved the idea and commissioned Howard to write an article combining the latest statistics, interviews with other small business owners, and her own story of building a business that gave her the freedom to divide her time between the city and a regional coastal town. As a result, she was invited to speak on multiple podcasts, her book is now available in many regional libraries, and she's been asked to run community workshops on how freelancers and solopreneurs can best grow their business to suit their lifestyle. Someone even sent her article to the local MP to take note of the growing trend. 'Finding a new take on a current topic, or a twist on the zeitgeist, really appeals to some editors and podcasters,' Howard says. 'It was also incredibly helpful to have two or three prepared talking points for interviews that related back to my objective of selling the book.'

If you feel confident in your writing ability, like Howard, you may want to pitch your article, research or story idea to a magazine/newspaper editor or TV/radio producer. Getting noticed among the 200–300 pitches in an editor's daily or weekly inbox is the first hurdle. This was the topic on a panel I moderated with *Good Weekend*'s Katrina Strickland, Officeworks' magazine content director Kate Barracosa and SBS Food online editor Farah Celjo. Their advice was invaluable.

The first tip was to read their magazines/platforms/podcasts and understand the sorts of stories they run. Ensure you spell the editor's name correctly. You'd be surprised how many don't. Keep your pitch short and snappy. All the editors agreed they prefer to receive pitches via email, not social media. And don't send a finished article; this might be a waste of your time and theirs. After pitching, if you don't hear back after a week, send a short enquiry.

If you are commissioned to write an article, keep to the brief. Don't send more words than required, and file before the deadline. If your idea is rejected, don't take it personally. It might be a great idea, but it may not fit the content mix that week or month. If you're promoting your book, service, cause, research or some other issue, it's possible you won't be paid for the article; however, the PR can be invaluable.

Karen Eck, PR strategist and founder of eckfactor and the Power of Visibility, has spent much of her professional life pitching stories to news editors, producers and journalists. Her three golden rules for successful pitches are:

- **Prepare**: Do your research on a journalist or potential client. Check out their social media, particularly LinkedIn, their websites and most recent work or news articles. Make sure what you're offering is relevant.
- **Precision**: Respect a journalist's or client's work schedule. Ask when it's convenient to speak and stick to that. Don't call them just before a deadline or on their day off.
- **Professionalism**: Be authentic and accept a 'no thanks' graciously. Building relationships is a long road.

If your idea isn't picked up, research alternative platforms. Think about where your audience is and be strategic about linking your offer to bigger topical issues, recent research or partnering with other parties. And don't discount the power of old-fashioned face-to-face networking.

This tactic has worked well for Jackie Baron, who's created an all-natural, Australian-made deodorant for teen boys. Her Neon Goat brand was inspired by a desire to combat her pubescent sons' body odour problem without nasty chemicals. She regularly sends media releases and product samples with different approaches to suit each platform. Her broad range of angles include female founder, boys' health and wellness, organic products and parenting. She even successfully pitched Neon Goat as part of an article on Christmas gift ideas to the *Weekend Australian* magazine. At a networking function, she met a Channel Seven news reporter and spruiked her product.

Later, when the reporter was doing a story on Australian Made Week, she rang Baron for an interview. Baron had her key messages ready: 'Neon Goat is all about backing boys, backing local, and building something that smells and feels good from the ground up.'

Another approach is to start your own Substack newsletter or pitch to one of its writers to interview you. Substack is a fast-growing writing platform featuring newsletters and blogs on a vast array of topics. Some content is free, although most is available to subscribers only. If you're an academic, you could pitch to *The Conversation*, an online publication written by academics and journalists. If you're a not-for-profit organisation, consider sitting on an expert panel, particularly if there will be philanthropists and policymakers in the audience.

Despite digital marketers claiming the media release is dead, it's still one of the best ways to reach the right journalist, editor or producer to pique their interest. Here's a template for a standard release, followed by the media release I wrote for the launch of Dogs Australia.

Date

MEDIA RELEASE

YOUR ATTENTION-GRABBING HEADLINE GOES HERE

If needed, add a subhead to support the headline

The first sentence contains the strongest news angle you have identified for your client or product. Journalists will decide whether they bother reading any further based on the strength of this opening paragraph.

The first and second paragraphs of the release should briefly answer all the key questions about your product, company or event (who, what, why, when, where and how). Journalists are short on time and will get frustrated if they have to go searching too far into the release for this information.

The rest of the release supports the opening paragraphs, expanding on the news angle with relevant facts and figures, quotes or background information. Journalists will probably only read this far if they are interested in your news angle.

- Bullet points can be a useful device in the body of releases because they allow you to abbreviate information.

- Make sure you include all the 'key messages' in your release.

- Keep the look of the release basic and business-like. Don't be overdramatic in your use of bold, all caps, large fonts or exclamation marks. Don't include graphics other than the company logo, and never make a news release look like a sales or marketing document – that's a big turn-off for journalists.

- Always proofread and spellcheck your document.

Most news releases contain a quote or two from a company or product spokesperson. This is an opportunity to signal to the media who might be available as 'talent' for an interview.

'Make sure you put quotation marks around all quotes and clearly identify the name and role of the spokesperson,' said TM Media director Theresa Miller. 'You should also use clear, simple language so quotes sound as natural as possible.'

Unless you are dealing with a highly sensitive or complex matter, most media releases should be kept to one page or two at the most.

Further information: your contact details (name, phone number and email) always go at the bottom of the release.

Add links to website, socials and media photos/videos.

Boilerplate description of your organisation, briefly explaining what you do.

MEDIA RELEASE

<u>DOGS AUSTRALIA: NEW TRICKS FOR OLD BREEDS</u>
-- Educating and Creating Communities Enriched by Dogs --

(Sydney, December 12, 2021) This week's launch of the not-for-profit organisation, **Dogs Australia**, coincides with a spike in dog ownership[1] and an eagerness to find the most suitable breeds from ethical breeders.

Dogs Australia is the new consumer face of the internationally recognised Australian National Kennel Council (ANKC) and unites the expertise of an estimated 60,000 members,[2] including 11,000 registered breeders, 350 breed clubs and almost 500 sports for dogs clubs across all states and territories.

"The launch of Dogs Australia draws on the strength and experience of all the state and territory-based member bodies to advocate for dog welfare and responsible dog ownership," said Dogs Australia President, Hugh Gent, OAM.

With a surge in dog ownership during lockdown and an alarming rise in online puppy scams, Dogs Australia is promoting the benefits of buying through its network of registered breeders.

"Our registered breeders follow a strict code of ethics, conduct health and DNA tests, provide a certificate of pedigree and give the owner on-going support," said Mr Gent. "Our breeders are passionate about finding the right homes for their dogs."

---

[1] Animal Medicines Australia

[2] Members including those of affiliated bodies

The rebranding of the 63-year-old ANKC includes the launch of a national education campaign in February to help potential dog owners find the most suitable breed to fit their family and lifestyle.

The campaign includes a video series showcasing more than 180 breeds categorised into seven distinct groups:
1) Toys
2) Terriers
3) Gundogs
4) Hounds
5) Working Dogs
6) Utility
7) Non-Sporting

"A dog is a big commitment. It should never be an impulse buy," said Dogs Australia ambassador and veterinarian, Dr Rob Zammit. "We recommend people thoroughly research their dog choice and they can start with our online questionnaire to determine whether it's the right time to buy a pup, which breed and breeder to choose."

Dogs Australia aims to safeguard the future of pedigree dogs through ethical breeding and canine health research while promoting conformation shows and sports for dogs that fulfil a breed's natural instincts.

For media enquiries: [Redacted]

Dogs Australia is a not-for-profit organisation advocating for the preservation of purebred dogs through ethical breeding.

Page 2

Once you've sent your media release to the right people, it's essential to follow up with a phone call to the journalist, TV/radio producer or podcaster to see if they'd like to use your story idea and interview you. If you get the green light, craft your key messages for the interview using the structures in chapter 3 and practise them out loud.

However, daunting it might seem, if you have a compelling story to tell that a certain audience needs to hear, you will find a way. Persistence outstrips all virtues. My sincere wish for you is that you will find something useful in this book to boost your confidence and skills to step up to the microphone and be heard. The right to free speech is not something to take for granted. Many people around the world are denied the right to speak out. Let's not squander our privilege. We are a richer and more informed society when we have a diverse chorus of expert and experienced voices.

If you have something important to say, don't stay silent. As legendary Canadian author Margaret Atwood once said: 'A voice is a human gift; it should be cherished and used … powerlessness and silence go together.' Good luck. I look forward to hearing what you have to say.

References

1 Why speak up?

Lintner, T & Belovecová, B, 'Demographic predictors of public speaking anxiety among university students', *Current Psychology*, vol. 43, 2024, pp. 25215–23.

Wallechinsky, D & Wallace, A, *The Book of Lists: The Original Compendium of Curious Information*, Allen & Unwin, Sydney, 2023, pp. 469–70.

3 Structuring your presentation

Banks, K, 'The Aboriginal knowledge stored in the stars', TEDxYouth@ Sydney, April 2019.

Brown, B, 'The power of vulnerability', TEDxHouston, June 2010.

Campbell, J, *The Hero with a Thousand Faces*, Pantheon Books, 1949.

Connolly, A, 'The invisible killer', *ABC Background Briefing*, 15 February 2025, <www.abc.net.au/listen/programs/backgroundbriefing/the-invisible-killer-01-aged-care-true-crime-healthcare-murder/104927502>.

Harari, YN, *21 Lessons for the 21st Century*, Jonathan Cape, London, 2018.

Pape, S, 'Diary of a bushfire victim', *Barefoot Investor*, 22 January 2020, <www.barefootinvestor.com/articles/diary-of-a-bushfire-victim>.

4 Body language and delivery

ABC News, '"Let there be a thousand blossoms bloom!" Bob Katter on same-sex marriage', *YouTube*, 29 November 2017, <https://www.youtube.com/watch?v=1i739SyCu9I>.

Mehrabian, A, *Silent Messages: Implicit Communication of Emotions and Attitudes*, Wadsworth Publishing Company, Belmont, 1971.

Özçalışkan, S, Lucero, C & Goldin-Meadow, S, 'Is seeing gesture necessary to gesture like a native speaker?', *Psychological Science*, vol. 27, no. 5, 2016, <pubmed.ncbi.nlm.nih.gov/26980154/>

Toastmasters International, <www.toastmasters.org>.

5 How to be a confident media spokesperson

Australian Communications and Media Authority, 'ACMA research reveals Australian news consumption trends', *Australian Communications and Media Authority*, 21 February 2024, <www.acma.gov.au/articles/2024-02/acma-research-reveals-australian-news-consumption-trends>.

Edelman, 'Edelman Trust Barometer 2025', *Edelman*, n.d., <www.edelman.com/trust/2025/trust-barometer>.

Kapadia, A [director], *2027*, Double Agent & Film4, 2024.

Kershaw, R, 'National Press Club address,' *National Intelligence Community*, 24 April 2024, <www.intelligence.gov.au/news/national-press-club-AFP-Commissioner>.

Lamble, S, *News As It Happens: An Introduction to Journalism*, Oxford University Press, Melbourne, 2016.

Newshounds, <www.squizkids.com.au/about-newshounds>.

Plain English Foundation, <www.plainenglishfoundation.com>.

Swan, E, 'Caught in a storm of misinformation, getting the right info is a disaster', *Sydney Morning Herald*, 13 March 2025, <http://www.smh.com.au/national/caught-in-a-storm-of-misinformation-getting-the-right-info-is-a-disaster-20250311-p5liqo.html>.

The Squiz, <thesquiz.com.au/>.

UNSW Sydney, 'Experts highlight urgent need to combat misinformation', *UNSW Sydney*, 17 October 2024, <www.unsw.edu.au/news/2024/10/Misinformation-in-the-media>.

Watson, D, *Worst Words: A Compendium of Contemporary Cant, Gibberish and Jargon*, Vintage, Melbourne, 2015.

Wren, T, 'Women's March 4 Justice and JobSeeker changes may seem worlds apart – but they're linked', *ABC News*, 15 March 2021, <www.abc.net.au/news/2021-03-15/jobkeeper-and-womens-march-4-justice-linked-poverty-violence/13248392?utm_source=abc_news_app&utm_medium=content_shared&utm_campaign=abc_news_app&utm_content=other>.

7 The power of inclusion

Australian Women Speakers, <womenspeakers.com.au>.

Chatfield, A, *It's a Lot* [podcast], <www.itsalotpodcast.com/>.

Ferguson, H & Adams, SJ, *Big Small Talk* [podcast], <mik.studio/project/big-small-talk>.

Media Diversity Australia, 'Who gets to tell Australian stories? 2.0', *Media Diversity Australia*, n.d., <www.mediadiversityaustralia.org/who-gets-to-tell-australian-stories-2-0/>.

Missing Perspectives, <missingperspectives.com>.

Notley, T & Dezuanni, M, 'On an average day, only 1% of Australian news stories quotes a young person. No wonder so few trust the media', *The Conversation*, 2 September 2019, <theconversation.com/on-an-average-day-only-1-of-australian-news-stories-quoted-a-young-person-no-wonder-so-few-trust-the-media-122464>.

Raise Our Voice Australia, <raiseourvoiceaustralia.com>.

University of Canberra, 'Digital News Report: Australia 2025', *University of Canberra*, n.d., <www.canberra.edu.au/research/centres/nmrc/digital-news-report-australia>.
Women in Media, 'Women are severely under-represented in Australian Media', *Women in Media*, 15 February 2023, <www.womeninmedia.com.au/post/women-are-severely-under-represented-in-australian-media>.

Conclusion: Making your voice heard
Atwood, M, 'A Disneyland of the soul', in Toronto Arts Group for Human Rights, *The Writer and Human Rights*, Anchor Press, Toronto, 1983, pp. 129–32.

Acknowledgements

Thank you to all the clever and generous people I interviewed for this book. Your insights and experience have been invaluable. In no particular order: Debra Cromer, Belinda Ferrari, Stephen Watson, John Demartini, Ronni Kahn, Sara Grafenauer, Tanna Bellear, Anne Connolly, Karen Eck, Rebecca Denholm, Meraiah Foley, Petra Buchanan, Shilpi Joshi, Samantha Theron, Lia Tsimos, Toni Wren, Candice Hughes, Mimi Zou, Jason Grebeley, Jessica Klein, David McLachlan, Robyn Sefiani, Sara Howard, Jackie Baron, Pranjali Sehgal and Ricky Kremer.

I'm forever indebted to Christopher Whitnall and David Borean who invited me to join talkforce as a presentation and media skills trainer, even before I knew what a corporate trainer was. You unlocked a whole new career for me, and your fundamental principles of clear communication, accelerated learning and respect for the different ways people process information have been life changing.

A big thank you to UNSW for giving me the opportunity to media train brilliant academics and help shine a light on their research. I have learned so much from each of them. In particular, thank you to Yolande Hutchinson from the media and communications team for making the process such a pleasure.

I'm so grateful to all the organisations who invite me into their boardrooms and meeting spaces to empower them to become better spokespeople. It takes courage to step out of your comfort zone, to be interviewed on camera and receive honest feedback.

Big hugs to my dear friend Karen Eck who always has my back and first persuaded me to write this book many summers ago when we walked along the Moonta Bay jetty in South Australia. Thank you also to Bernadette Schwerdt for urging me to keep writing, and to Laura Templin for encouraging me to see the big picture.

To my assistant, Brooke Schoenman, I really appreciate you for keeping the wheels turning at TM Media while I focused on this book.

Many thanks to Elspeth Menzies at NewSouth Publishing for taking onboard this idea so readily and enthusiastically. And thank you to Gabrielle Sterio whose professional editing has made this a better book.

Take a bow, Thérèse Leuver for your eye-catching cover design. You are a joy to work with. I'm also indebted to the first readers who wrote endorsements for *Speak Up* – your support means everything to me.

Last but not least, thank you to my family – to Stuart for loving and supporting me unconditionally and making me laugh every day. And to my inspirational daughters Zoe and Sienna: I never tire of hearing you speak up. I love you and am so proud of you.

Index